DIGITAL LIFE SKILLS FOR TEENS

The Essential Digital Survival Guide

How to Communicate, Behave, Stay Safe and Find Balance in an Online World

FERNE BOWE

View all our books at **bemberton.com**

CONTENTS

INTRODUCTION

What kinds of skills do you think are most important and useful for people today? There are the basics, like reading, writing, and mental arithmetic — these skills remain as crucial as ever. But, alongside these old favorites, a whole new set of skills has emerged that are fundamental for thriving in the modern environment. They're called digital skills.

WHAT ARE DIGITAL SKILLS?

The term "digital skills" refers to the skills that people use online (when connected to the Internet) or when using their electronic devices (cell phones, laptops, tablets, etc.). It covers everything from learning the rules of online etiquette to knowing how to search effectively and understanding how to stay safe and secure online. These skills have become central to daily life over the past few decades, and are likely to become even more important in the future.

If you think about how often you reach for your computer or a device to look up or check in on your friends, and how much of your schoolwork and leisure time involves using an electronic screen, you'll begin to understand how vital these skills are.

A TOOLKIT FOR THE MODERN WORLD

The reasons to develop your digital skills are many and varied. From using software to submit your homework on time to accessing your money, life is easier when you know how to work with technology. But staying safe online, avoiding scams, navigating different online spaces, and getting the most out of the Internet when searching or shopping takes practice. No one is born knowing this stuff!

This book is your guide to essential digital skills that will stay with you for life. It covers:

- The history of digital communication

- How to stay safe online

- Etiquette in online spaces

- Developing strong communication skills

- Techniques for finding exactly what you need online

- Tips for secure online shopping

- Strategies for balancing your online and offline lives

How to Use This Book

This book is designed to be flexible, so you can use it however works best for you. Whether that means reading it cover-to-cover or dipping in and out as topics become relevant, it's up to you. Keep it around when you spend time online, in case you want to check or reference something. You might also find it helpful to share some of the ideas with your parents, other trusted adults, and your friends.

By the end of the book, you'll have a good understanding of a wide range of digital skills and how and when to use them. You'll be able to send an email without stress, find exactly what you're looking for in a sea of search results, and spot fake news like a pro. You'll also find valuable tips on how to stay healthy mentally and physically in an increasingly digital world, plus some bonus ideas about useful life skills, such as budgeting.

Let's get to it! Your voyage of digital discovery starts here.

BEMBERTON
BOOKS

 # SOMETHING
FOR YOU

Thanks for buying this book. To show our appreciation, here's a **FREE** printable copy of the "Life Skills for Tweens Workbook"

WITH OVER 80 FUN ACTIVITIES **JUST FOR TWEENS!**

Scan the code to download your FREE printable copy

1

THE DIGITAL EVOLUTION: HOW TECHNOLOGY TRANSFORMED OUR LIVES

Can you imagine a world without computers? It's hard to picture, right? But believe it or not, there was a time before Alexa could play you a song, before Google was the go-to resource for research, and when you had to wait until the end of a film to learn an actor's name.

Now, these things are everyday essentials. But while it can feel like computers and mobile devices have been around forever, their rapid advancement is relatively recent. Let's rewind and see how it all started.

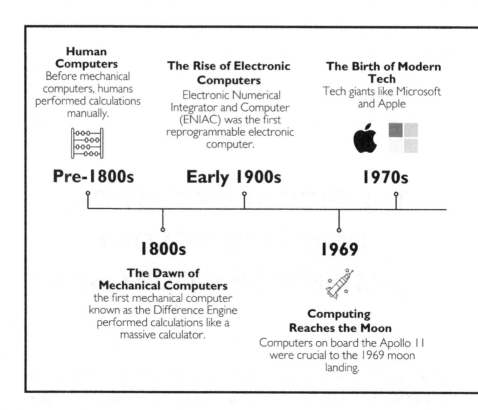

Human Computers
Before mechanical computers, humans performed calculations manually.

The Rise of Electronic Computers
Electronic Numerical Integrator and Computer (ENIAC) was the first reprogrammable electronic computer.

The Birth of Modern Tech
Tech giants like Microsoft and Apple

Pre-1800s

Early 1900s

1970s

1800s

The Dawn of Mechanical Computers
the first mechanical computer known as the Difference Engine performed calculations like a massive calculator.

1969

Computing Reaches the Moon
Computers on board the Apollo 11 were crucial to the 1969 moon landing.

A Brief History of Computing

It's not possible to cover every advance in computing here, but this timeline should help you get a general idea of the developments over the years.

Pre-1800s: Human Computers

The word "computer" comes from the Latin word "putare," meaning "to think" and "to prune." Add "com," meaning "together," and you get "computare," meaning "to calculate."

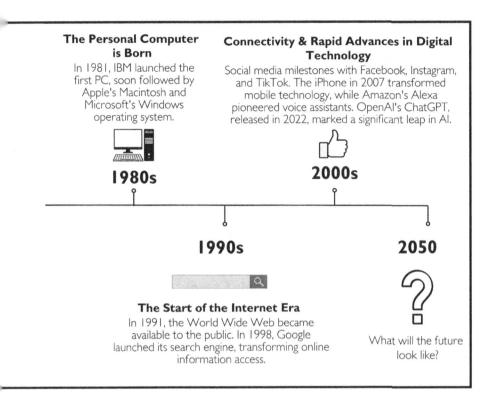

The Personal Computer is Born

In 1981, IBM launched the first PC, soon followed by Apple's Macintosh and Microsoft's Windows operating system.

1980s

Connectivity & Rapid Advances in Digital Technology

Social media milestones with Facebook, Instagram, and TikTok. The iPhone in 2007 transformed mobile technology, while Amazon's Alexa pioneered voice assistants. OpenAI's ChatGPT, released in 2022, marked a significant leap in AI.

2000s

1990s

The Start of the Internet Era

In 1991, the World Wide Web became available to the public. In 1998, Google launched its search engine, transforming online information access.

2050

What will the future look like?

Humans did all the calculations in the olden days, and the word "computer" referred to mathematicians.

The 1800s: The Dawn of Mechanical Computers

In the 1820s, long before electricity or the invention of the telephone, British inventor Charles Babbage designed the first mechanical computer. Known as the Difference Engine, this steam-powered device performed calculations like a massive calculator.

Early 1900s: The Rise of Electronic Computers

Fast forward a century and meet the Electronic Numerical Integrator and Computer (ENIAC). Completed in 1945 for the US Army, this giant was the first reprogrammable electronic computer. It was as big as a house and weighed 30 tons!

To put that into perspective, 30 tons is about the weight of six African elephants!

1969: Computing Reaches the Moon

The year 1969 was a monumental one for technology. The Apollo Guidance Computer on board Apollo 11 was integral to the 1969 moon landing, despite having less computing power than a modern smartphone.

The 1970s: The Birth of the Modern Tech Giants

The late 1970s saw the rise of companies like Apple and Microsoft, marking the beginning of widespread home and personal computing.

From the 1980s to Today: The Personal Computer Revolution

In the 1980s, computers started to become a part of everyday life. Here's a (very) brief look at some of the big events:

- 1981: IBM introduces the personal computer ("PC" for short).

- 1984: Apple launches the Macintosh.

- 1985: Microsoft releases its Windows operating system.

- 1991: The World Wide Web becomes available to the public.

- 1998: Google launches Google Search.

- 2004: The launch of Facebook.

- 2007: Release of the first iPhone.

- 2010: Instagram comes online.

- 2014: Amazon introduces Alexa with the Echo.

- 2016: TikTok launches, rapidly gaining popularity.

- 2022: OpenAI releases the first version of ChatGPT.

- 2050: What will the future look like?

What This Means for You: The Importance of Staying Updated

Advances in technology bring more possibilities and drive down the cost of tech. However, these advances also mean that devices like smartphones and tablets now only have a short lifespan, and people feel that they have to replace their devices regularly to keep up (not great for the planet or the pocketbook!).

It's not just the devices that evolve — so do the platforms. For instance, TikTok reached 100 million users in only nine months. Because things move so quickly, it can be a challenge to keep up. That's why it's important to develop digital skills early and keep them sharp throughout our lives.

Digital Skills: The New Language of Our Times

Digital skills are crucial. They extend beyond how to use devices, apps, and the Internet to understanding how to use them responsibly and make smart choices.

Developing these skills is like learning a new language or mastering a musical instrument. It requires regular practice to stay up-to-date, especially as technology evolves.

A Day in the Life: Digital Skills in Action

To illustrate the importance of tech, let's imagine a typical day for a digitally connected person:

TIME	ACTIVITY
7:05 am	Wakes up with a smartphone alarm.
7:20 am	Asks Alexa to play a favorite song.
8:00 am	Messages a friend.
8:15 am	Browses social media over breakfast.
10:30 am	Researches online for a school project.
Noon	Organizes homework schedule in a digital planner.
2:30 pm	Messages parent for a ride home.
4:30 pm	Plays Fortnite with friends.
6:15 pm	Completes homework and submits it online.
7:30 pm	Watches a show on Netflix.
9:00 pm	Listens to an audiobook with a sleep timer.

This is just a snapshot — not every young person lives like this. But it highlights our increasing reliance on technology.

Why Digital Skills Matter

Digital skills are as essential as reading and math to help us navigate our digital world. Whether at home, school, or work, technology is part of almost every aspect of our lives, from streaming movies to completing homework online.

TECHNOLOGY IN THE WORKPLACE

"Computer science empowers students to create the world of tomorrow." — Satya Nadella, CEO of Microsoft

Technology has changed the way we work. It's created new jobs (like app developers and social media influencers), and almost every job requires some digital skills (whether basic typing or more advanced skills like coding).

In the next chapter, we will explore how to build these skills and stay safe.

UNDERSTANDING DIGITAL SAFETY: HOW TO PROTECT YOURSELF ONLINE

The Internet is full of exciting opportunities. It's a portal to a world of knowledge, a platform for innovation and creativity, a window to limitless entertainment, and a place for connecting with friends and family. But it also presents potential risks. Understanding and navigating these hazards is what digital safety is all about.

What Is Digital Safety?

You've probably heard of "digital safety," also known as e-safety, online safety, or Internet safety. But what does it really mean?

Simply put, digital safety is about protecting yourself and your personal information in the online world. It's learning how to balance the resources and connections the Internet offers with the need to protect your digital identity and personal data.

Just as you wouldn't share personal details with a stranger on the street, you need to be cautious about what you share online, and with whom.

What Is Personal Data?

Think of personal data as your digital fingerprint. It's information that identifies you, including your name, address, school, and even your interests. This data is as valuable as gold for companies and advertisers. They use it to target you with their services and ads. There are two main ways your data can be shared:

1. **Voluntary Sharing:** This is when you share information publicly, such as when you post on social media, sign up for a new app, or enter your details into a shopping website.

2. **Involuntary Collection:** This is when sites or apps collect data about you without you actively giving it to them. They do this through cookies or tracking your activities online, like the posts you like.

Digital Safety Skills

Developing strong digital safety skills will set you up for successful and safe online experiences. In this chapter, we'll look at some things to be aware of and some ways to protect yourself online.

THE IMPORTANCE OF PROTECTING PERSONAL DATA

Companies using your personal data to sell you things might not sound too bad. However, once your data is out there, you have no control over it. Companies can change their terms or even sell your data to other parties, who might have different ideas about what to do with it.

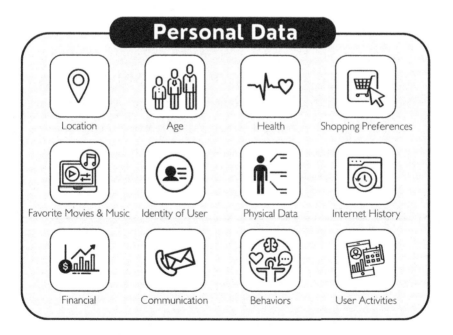

Most social media platforms, like Facebook, Instagram, and TikTok, collect user information for advertising. When you create an account on these platforms, you agree to their terms and conditions, often allowing them to monitor your activities on their site.

What Kind of Information Do They Collect?

Think about the things you do on social media — those times you looked up an old friend or joined a group, or those direct messages where you shared personal experiences. All of these are tracked and recorded anonymously against your user ID.

Why Do They Collect This Information?

You might wonder why social media platforms are interested in these details. The answer is simple: It's all about creating a detailed profile of you. This profile isn't just a list of your likes and dislikes — it's a comprehensive picture of your interests, habits, and preferences. By understanding who you are, these platforms can tailor advertisements specifically to you, making them more effective and, ultimately, more profitable.

Your personal information is also highly attractive to hackers and scammers. If they get hold of it, they can try to "steal" your identity. Sounds impossible, right? After all, you're unique! However, identity theft is a very real and very serious issue. It occurs when someone uses your personal details without your consent, potentially opening bank accounts or applying for loans in your name.

The consequences of identity theft can be severe, impacting your future and leading to financial difficulties. Unfortunately, many victims of identity theft remain unaware of how their information was taken, and resolving these issues can be both stressful and costly.

What Is a Hacker?

The term "hacker" refers to someone using computer programming skills to illegally access another person's computer system. Once inside, they can access, retrieve, or manipulate any information stored on the system. This could range from personal data, like emails and photographs, to more sensitive details, including financial information.

The Threat of Online Predators

Sharing personal information publicly, whether on purpose or by accident, can expose you to the risk of online predators. These individuals often create fake social media profiles to make themselves seem legitimate and hide their predatory behavior. They might use convincingly real or AI-generated profile pictures and slang to pretend to have interests that make them seem like young people.

Unfortunately, these people's intentions are rarely good. They might try to manipulate their victims into giving away personal information in order to steal money, or they might try to get victims to do dangerous things, like sending intimate photographs or meeting up in person. Sometimes, predators offer gifts or money to establish "trusting relationships." They can be very convincing and may work on a victim for months or even years.

It's crucial to remember that people you meet online are strangers, regardless of how friendly they may seem. Tell a trusted adult immediately if an online interaction feels suspicious.

How to Protect Your Personal Data: Essential Tips for Online Safety

Just like in the offline world, there are some simple steps that you can take to stay as safe as possible online.

1. Guard your personal information.

Would you share your deepest secrets with a stranger you met on the street? Probably not! The same caution should apply online. Always remember that your personal information should remain just that — personal. Never share sensitive details on the Internet with people you don't know.

2. Create strong passwords.

One of the most effective methods to protect your personal information is to use strong, unique passwords for each account. Avoid copying and pasting passwords. When you copy a password, it's stored in the clipboard, which can be accessed by any application with permission, potentially exposing your password.

Remember, sharing passwords, even with friends, is a risky move. Once a password is shared, you lose control over how and when it is used or who else it might be passed to.

Passwords to Avoid

A good password should be unique, complex, and hard to guess. A bad password is the opposite! Here are some examples of bad passwords to avoid:

- **Simple number sequences:** "123456" is a classic example of an incredibly easy-to-crack password. It's just a simple sequence of numbers.

- **Default passwords:** Using "password" as your password is as bad as not having one. It's one of the first guesses a hacker will make.

- **Keyboard patterns:** "qwerty" might seem clever, as it follows the top row of letters on the keyboard, but it's far from secure.

- **Repeated numbers with slight variations:** Using a short sequence like "11111" or "123123" is also risky, as it's simple and repetitive.

- **Personal information:** Passwords based on personal information, like birthdays, your address, or family member names, are easy to work out, especially with the amount of personal data available online.

3. Explore privacy settings.

Many users, including adults, are unaware you can adjust the privacy settings for devices, apps, and websites. Those cookies that websites keep asking about? Declining them can prevent the site from collecting and selling your information to third parties (usually advertisers). Customizing these settings takes a little time, but it's a valuable step in controlling who sees what about you.

What Are Cookies?

Cookies on your computers are a little different from the ones you eat! They are small files that sites place on your digital device to store information (such as your login information), so you don't have to sign in every time you visit. They also track what you look at, what pages you visit, and what you click on. Companies use this information to show you more relevant information and content. However, it's also sold to advertisers so they can target you with ads that match your interests.

4. Use a VPN.

A virtual private network (VPN) is an essential tool for online privacy. Just like an envelope protects the contents of a letter, a VPN shields your browsing activity, identity, and location.

It hides your IP address — your device's online ID that can reveal your physical location — safeguarding any personal data you transmit online.

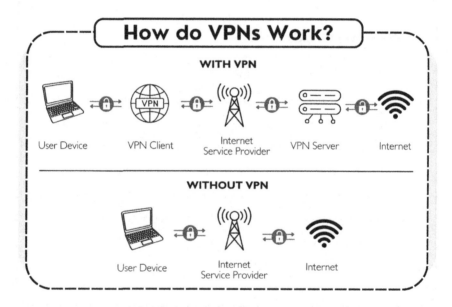

Online Scams: A Guide to Staying Safe on the Internet

Imagine this: You're online and come across something that seems important, like a message from your bank asking for your account details or a notification telling you you've won a prize for a competition you don't remember entering. You quickly enter your details, but something feels off. The "bank's" website doesn't look quite right...

You've just fallen for an online scam.

WHAT IS AN ONLINE SCAM?

Online scams are clever tricks used by certain people on the Internet to fool you into giving them your personal information, or even your money. They take many forms and are often very convincing.

Scams are designed to look real, making it hard to tell them apart from genuine interactions. Scammers use cleverly disguised emails, phone calls, images, or messages to mislead you into thinking they're someone they're not.

Even if you're smart with technology, online scams can still catch you out. Scammers use tricky methods to deceive you into revealing personal information, sending money, or downloading harmful software that can steal your data, including private details.

The Different Types of Scams

There are many different online scams, and scammers constantly develop new methods as people become aware of the threats. Some examples of common scams include:

- **Phishing scams:** Scammers try to get you to give away personal information they can use for further scam activity.

- **Ransomware/scareware scams:** Clicking a link or downloading a file locks up or threatens to damage your computer unless a ransom is paid.

- **Friend/romance scams:** Scammers pretend to be interested in friendship or a romantic relationship to get money or information.

- **Money transfer scams:** Scammers attempt to get you to send them money by pretending to be bank employees, family members, or even foreign dignitaries.

- **Lottery scams:** A notice that you've won a competition or lottery takes you to a page where all the data you input is taken by scammers.

Scammers use technology to convince their victims that they're real. Email, telephone, chat apps, and social media are all common avenues of attack.

Email

Beware of emails claiming to be from your bank or other trusted organizations. They might ask you to click a link and provide account details or other personal information. These emails are not actually from the organization they say they are! They're from scammers trying to lure you into clicking links or responding, with the aim of stealing your information or accessing your bank account.

Telephone

Scammers also use phone calls, pretending to be from banks or other organizations. Their goal is similar: to get you to give away your personal details, usually so they can steal your money. If you suspect a phone scam, hang up immediately. You can always call the organization back using a trusted phone number.

Chat and Social Media

Scammers often use social media messages or apps like WhatsApp and iMessage. They send messages that appear to be from sources like PayPal or your bank, asking you to click a link or share personal information.

Scam Protection Tips

BE CAUTIOUS WITH UNEXPECTED CONTACTS
Don't click suspicious links. Verify with the organization directly.

SAFEGUARD YOUR INFORMATION
Never share personal details via email or phone. Legitimate organizations won't pressure you.

EXAMINE EMAIL DETAILS
Look for mistakes or oddities in email addresses and domains.

TRUST YOUR GUT
If something feels off, it probably is. Avoid suspicious links and offers.

STAY UP-TO-DATE
Learn about new scam tactics and stay skeptical.

DON'T RUSH
Scammers create urgency. Stop, think, and verify.

PROTECT YOUR DEVICES
Use antivirus software and firewalls. Be careful with downloads.

MAKE REGULAR BACK-UPS
Keep important data backed up to prevent loss from theft, damage, or viruses.

Tips to Protect Yourself from Scams

Scammers are always devising new ways to trick people, using sophisticated methods that can be hard to spot. But there are ways to protect yourself and stay safe, even as scams become more advanced.

1. **Be cautious with unexpected contacts**: If you receive a message or email from someone you don't know or a message that just doesn't feel right, don't click on any links. You can always double-check by contacting the organization's official contact.

2. **Examine email details**: Pay attention to the small things. Scam emails might have mistakes or seem a bit off. For example, the email address might look weird or not match the sender's name. Look out for letters replaced with numbers ("PayPa1," for example) or odd domain names.

3. **Safeguard your information**: Your personal details, like passwords and bank info, are precious. Never share them via email or phone call. If someone pressures you, hang up or don't respond. No legitimate representative of an organization will attempt to pressure you into giving away your details.

4. **Don't rush**: Scammers love to create a sense of urgency so their victims don't get a chance to stop and think. They might tell you an offer is only good right then to rush you into a decision or that someone is hacking your bank account

and they need to move your money to safety immediately. Remember, real opportunities don't need you to decide in a panic! Stop, hang up, and think.

5. **Protect your devices:** Use antivirus software and keep your computer's firewall on. These are your digital shields against unwanted intruders. Be aware of what you're downloading and from where—free online "goodies" are often nasties in disguise. "Free" items frequently come with a hidden price tag—often in the form of viruses or data harvesting by scammers.

6. **Trust your gut:** If something feels weird or too good to be true, it often is. Trust your instincts—if you're unsure about a link or an offer, it's better to be safe and avoid it. You can find lots of information about scams online, so do a quick search if you feel something is wrong.

7. **Stay up-to-date**: Scammers are quick to use the latest tech, like AI, for bad purposes. They might use AI to create fake videos (deepfakes) or to imitate someone you trust. So, it's important to keep learning and aware of the latest trends. Most importantly, always keep a healthy dose of skepticism. If something doesn't feel right, take a step back and think about it before acting.

8. **Make regular backups:** Always keep a backup of your important data and files. Whether it's to a physical external drive or cloud storage, having a backup means that if your device gets lost, stolen, damaged, or if you're hit by a virus, you won't lose everything.

Cyberbullying: Understanding and Tackling Digital Harassment

Cyberbullying, or online bullying, is an unfortunate reality in the digital world. It can happen anywhere online — through texts, social media, forums, or gaming platforms. Unlike offline bullying, cyberbullying doesn't happen face-to-face, although it can certainly spill over into the offline world.

What Is Cyberbullying?

Cyberbullying can take many forms. Some of the most common include:

- Sending rude or hateful direct messages (DMs) or messages in group chats.

- Deliberately excluding someone from group chats.

- Posting hateful or rude comments about someone on social media.

- Circulating embarrassing or inappropriate images of someone on social media, email, or through messages.

- Tagging someone in offensive content, such as nasty memes, with the intention of upsetting them.

Cyberbullying can happen at any time of day or night, and bullies can share materials (such as fake videos or doctored photos) widely and quickly. When you combine this with the "always online" nature of modern life, cyberbullying can be difficult to escape.

The intent of cyberbullies is often to be hurtful, spread hate, or cause public humiliation to their victims. Sometimes, though, people don't realize that their behavior is bullying. It's important to think carefully about your actions online and their potential consequences.

The Internet can sometimes be like a mask, making bullies feel they can be mean without getting caught because they're hidden behind a screen. They don't see how their words or actions hurt someone, which might make them think it's okay to be unkind.

The reality is very different. Being mean online is never okay. It's just as bad as any other type of bullying. It can really hurt people, making them feel alone, sad, or even scared. Just because it happens online doesn't make it any less serious.

How to Deal with Cyberbullying

If you encounter online bullying, it's crucial to have strategies to deal with it:

- **Block the bully:** Immediately block the individual responsible for cyberbullying on the platform where it occurred.

- **Report the behavior:** Use the platform's reporting feature to report the cyberbully's actions.

- **Tell someone**: Talk about the situation with a trusted adult, such as a parent, teacher, or family member. There are also some useful resources at *www.stopbullying.gov*.

- **Involve your school:** Remember that teachers and school counselors can help, even if the bullying happens outside school hours.

Remember, you are not alone. Cyberbullying is serious, and you don't have to face it by yourself. Speaking up is a brave and important step towards stopping it.

Mobile Device Safety

With so many young people using cell phones these days, learning how to do so safely is key. Let's look at how you can enjoy your mobile device, stay safe, and keep your personal data private.

What Is Geolocation?

Geolocation, or GPS, is a feature that pinpoints your exact location. It's convenient for finding your way on a map or locating the nearest supermarket. However, this convenience comes with privacy risks.

Social media apps like Snapchat often allow you to share your location with others. While this feature can make it easy and fun to meet up with friends or check where they are, it can also expose your location to strangers.

Before you turn on geolocation, it's always best to check with your parents and limit sharing to your closest friends and contacts. Never share your location openly or with people you don't know well offline.

Photo Sharing and Geolocation

Photos are a big part of modern cell phone use. From capturing funny moments to asking a parent about a product or simply using fun filters for selfies, we take a lot of pictures!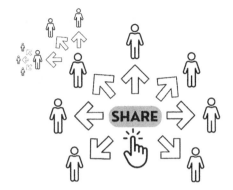

However, with geolocation, photos posted publicly can give away a lot of information about where you live, the school you attend, and where you like to hang out. This might not seem like a big deal, but it's information predators can use to find you or use against you. The more information predators have about you, the easier for them to convince you they're harmless.

Personal and Sensitive Images

If you share a photo online, it's out there forever and can quickly slip out of your control. It could be saved, forwarded, or even posted elsewhere by someone else, potentially making it impossible to remove entirely. This is particularly true for photos that contain nudity or other sensitive content, as they can lead to uncomfortable, embarrassing, or even harmful situations. They might be used in ways you never intended, affecting your privacy and well-being.

Tips on Sharing Photos Responsibly

1. **Pay attention to what's in your photos.** This includes identifying features of your location that could inadvertently reveal where you are. Also, don't include people who haven't consented to be in your photo.

2. **Watch what you wear.** If you wear a school uniform, think twice before sharing a photo of it publicly, as it can reveal where you go to school.

3. **Check before you share.** Double-check photos for any personal information before sharing them online. This includes visible school names, signs, or other sensitive information.

4. **Turn off automatic geotagging.** Check the settings for your social media accounts and turn off auto-tagging. If you're unsure how to do this, a simple online search like "How to turn off photo geotagging on [social media platform name]" can guide you.

5. **Share photos and your location only with people you know and trust.** Avoid broadcasting your location to a broad audience you don't know personally.

6. Be careful who you befriend. Only connect with people you know in real life.

7. Check which apps are using your geolocation. In settings, go to app permissions and check which apps use your location.

8. Turn off geolocation. This will also improve your battery life!

Handling Pressure and Saying No

If anyone pressures you to share images that make you uncomfortable, trust your instincts and say no. You have every right to protect your privacy and personal boundaries. If something doesn't feel right, you should always feel able to refuse and end the conversation. Remember, your comfort and safety should always come first.

Even if you don't feel uncomfortable sharing photos, you should still exercise common sense. Don't send private or sensitive photos to anyone — doing so can have enormous unintended consequences for you and the person you send them to.

Seeking Help When You Need It

If you feel uncomfortable or unsafe because of photos or requests for photos, it's essential to seek help immediately. Talk to a trusted adult, such as a parent, teacher, or school counselor. They can offer support and help you navigate the situation safely and respectfully.

All About Passwords

Creating strong passwords is your first line of defense in the digital world. Strong passwords act like fortified gates, keeping scammers and digital intruders at bay. Try this activity to help you understand what makes a strong password and how to create a secure and memorable one.

Step 1: Identifying Weak Passwords

First, examine the following list of passwords. Use a pen to circle the ones that might be easy for someone to guess:

1. password123

2. 50!!&*myjuice<99

3. 123456789

4. qwertyuiop

5. SigJ$>99!

Passwords are often vulnerable if they use common phrases, predictable letter patterns, or lack complexity. The best passwords incorporate a diverse mix of letters, symbols, numbers, and both uppercase and lowercase letters, and are impossible to guess.

Step 2: Creating a Strong Password

Now, let's craft a strong and memorable password for you. Follow these steps:

1. **Choose a base word:** Write down the name of your favorite animal or pet.

2. **Add a favorite thing:** Write down something that your chosen animal loves.

3. **Incorporate a number:** Write down your age or another memorable number.

4. **Mix it up:** Add an uppercase letter and one symbol.

5. **Combine elements:** Now, merge all these elements to form a unique sentence or string.

Example:
- Pet's name: Tag
- Loves: Cats
- Age: 10
- Uppercase and symbol: T and !
- Password: TagLovesCats10!

By using a blend of letters (both uppercase and lowercase), numbers, and symbols and ensuring the password is long, you can make it much tougher for someone to guess or crack your password.

Your Turn:

Now it's time for you to create your strong password. Follow the steps above and craft a password that's uniquely yours and tough to crack. If you don't have a pet, you can use some other person or thing in your life. Remember, a strong password is like a strong lock — it's a fundamental part of being safe and secure online.

- Pet's name: _____
- Loves: _____
- Age: _____
- Uppercase and symbol: _____

🔒 **PASSWORD:** _____

DIGITAL CONDUCT: HOW TO BEHAVE RESPONSIBLY ONLINE

The Internet is constantly evolving, and we're still figuring out how to make it safe and useful for everyone. Each of us has a role to play in this process, learning and adapting as we go.

Navigating the Online World

As a young person, understanding how to behave online is a huge part of learning to live in the world.

WHAT IS ONLINE BEHAVIOR?

Online behavior is the way people act and the things they do online. Similar to offline behavior, our online actions and behaviors can have a big impact on our lives and the lives of those around us.

Offline, the consequences are usually good when we help others. Helping a neighbor find their lost cat brings smiles all around — the neighbor is happy, we're happy, and even the cat is happy! On the other hand, negative actions have consequences, too. They can lead to guilt or even trouble with teachers or parents.

WHY DOES ONLINE BEHAVIOR MATTER?

Part of learning to live in the world with others is understanding our behavior's effects on them. It's normal to make mistakes, and no one always gets it right. When we're face-to-face with people, we see the consequences of our actions. We have thousands of years of culture to guide us, and we can learn the rules from one another.

Online, things aren't always so simple.

Our online behavior has just as much of an impact as our offline behavior, but it's not always as easy to see its effects. Hiding behind a screen can make it seem like there are no consequences, but that's not true. How we conduct ourselves online can have far-reaching effects on our relationships, careers, and opportunities.

How Can We Navigate Online Behavior?

Although the online space is fairly new, and we're still working things out, there are accepted ways of behaving online that are useful to know. In this chapter, we'll look at how to navigate the online world safely and responsibly.

We'll explore:

- The ins and outs of "netiquette"

- How to manage your digital footprint

- How to use social media so it's safe and fun for everybody

Netiquette 101

Etiquette is all about the rules we use to behave properly in situations and around others. Netiquette is the same, only on the Internet. Just like when we are offline, different parts of the online world have slightly different rules. But there are a few basic rules that apply pretty much everywhere. Knowing them means we'll have a much better time online, as will everyone around us.

Understanding Netiquette

Netiquette, like traditional etiquette, has evolved over time and continues to develop as we adapt to new forms of digital communication.

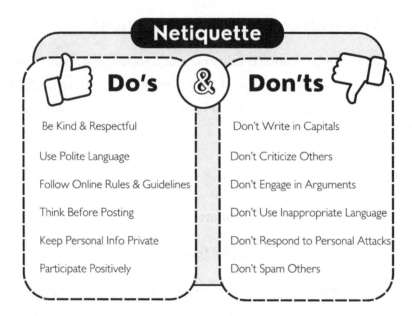

Netiquette

Do's & Don'ts

Do's	Don'ts
Be Kind & Respectful	Don't Write in Capitals
Use Polite Language	Don't Criticize Others
Follow Online Rules & Guidelines	Don't Engage in Arguments
Think Before Posting	Don't Use Inappropriate Language
Keep Personal Info Private	Don't Respond to Personal Attacks
Participate Positively	Don't Spam Others

People don't behave the same way today as they did 200 years ago. Over time, what has been considered good or bad manners has changed. For instance, while you might get scolded for talking with your mouth full today, 19th century table manners accepted different behaviors. Similarly, the way a 19th century teenager interacted with their best friend was very different from how they would behave with a school teacher.

However, how we behave today isn't completely different from the past. Some actions are just as unacceptable now as they were 100 years ago. The same goes for online behavior. We've established rules that adapt to different situations, but some actions remain inappropriate or are considered bad manners.

Just like in the offline world, practicing good manners online helps things run smoothly and ensures people are treated fairly. Misunderstandings are less likely when people agree on what constitutes good behavior.

We are all responsible for how we act online, making it crucial to learn and practice good netiquette.

Practicing Good Netiquette

Think about some of the social rules you follow in daily life. These likely include using polite phrases like "please" and "thank you," not interrupting people when they speak, and taking good care of items you borrow. While these rules might differ slightly depending on where you are, the basics apply everywhere and are important to master.

The same applies online. Here are some basic netiquette rules to help you navigate any online space.

Having Respect

- **Be kind:** Treat others online with the same courtesy and kindness as offline. Think about how you would like to be treated, then do that.

- **Keep it clean:** Use polite language that won't offend. Don't swear or call people names, even if you're joking.

- **Mind your tone:** Things don't always come across how you mean them to, especially when you are online. Try to be clear, direct, and polite in your interactions to avoid misunderstandings. Use emojis to make your meaning crystal clear.

- **Practice patience:** Remember that everyone communicates differently and has different strengths. Avoid correcting people's word choice, grammar, or spelling unless they ask you to.

Online Communities

- **Learn the rules:** When you join an online community, it will have a specific set of rules. Read them before engaging so you don't accidentally make a mistake.

- **Acknowledge others:** If someone asks you a reasonable question, reply honestly and in a friendly way. If you share someone else's work, make sure you credit them. That means adding their name when you share the work and not pretending it's your own.

- **Participate positively:** Aim to bring something good to the community you're taking part in. Offer helpful suggestions and share supportive comments where you can.

- **Take a moment to think:** Before you publish that post or send that comment, seriously consider any possible effects it could have — both on you and other people.

Identifying and Avoiding Negative Behavior

Not everyone follows good netiquette online. Similar to everyday life, some people like to cause trouble on the Internet for various reasons. Others may not realize their actions are disruptive, but the effect is often the same — people feel upset or hurt.

How to Spot Bad Behavior

Bad online behavior is often pretty easy to spot. Examples might include:

- Using inappropriate language

- Telling lies about another person or group

- Ganging up on one person or group

- Posting content that is intended to upset or hurt people

If you see these things happening online, it's important to take action. Remember, acting means reporting the behavior through the proper channels. Don't try to take on the perpetrators yourself!

What Is a Troll?

A troll is someone who purposely annoys or upsets other people. Sometimes trolls act this way because they find it funny, and other times they have nastier motives. Whatever their reasons, trolls want to provoke a reaction, and thrive on attention. Unfortunately, trolls are very common online. The only effective way to deal with them is to ignore, block, and report them.

TROLLS

WORLD OVER

- DO NOT FEED
- IGNORE
- DELETE
- BLOCK
- REPORT

TIPS TO DEAL WITH BAD BEHAVIOR ONLINE

Dealing with poor online behavior is an unfortunate reality, but it doesn't have to spoil your online experience. Here are some strategies to help you deal with negative behavior effectively.

1. **Keep your cool:** Don't get drawn into arguments or let people provoke you into responding. Breathe and take some offline time if you need to.

2. **Ignore trolls:** Trolls thrive on attention. Ignoring their comments or behavior can often defuse the situation and deny them the desired reaction.

3. **Rock that block button:** You're not obligated to engage with anyone. If someone is misbehaving, don't be afraid to block them. Most online platforms have this functionality, so use it!

4. **Report abuse:** If you see harassment, threats, or other forms of abusive behavior happening in an online space, report it to the platform administrators. Reporting abuse is anonymous, so don't be afraid that it will come back on you.

5. **Get help:** Tell someone if you're struggling with bad behavior online. Friends, family, and trusted adults can all help support you if things get unpleasant online.

6. **Document the evidence:** If you encounter negative behavior online, it's important to keep a record. Saving messages and taking screenshots can be helpful if you need to take action.

7. **Take breaks:** Taking occasional breaks from social media and other online platforms is always a good idea. By giving yourself breathing space outside of these platforms, you can prioritize your mental health and well-being.

Recognizing and Dealing with Harmful Content

Wherever you go online, there's a risk of encountering harmful content. Knowing how to respond can sometimes be challenging, but it is important to take action. It's down to all of us to create and maintain an online world in which everyone feels safe and comfortable.

REPORTING HARMFUL CONTENT

Like other forms of negative online behavior, the best way to handle harmful content is to report it. Most online platforms have a reporting system, but it's not always obvious what to do. If you're unsure how to report harmful content on a specific platform, try searching online for "how to report harmful content on [platform]."

It's important to remember that reporting content is anonymous, and you won't get in trouble or face any repercussions. Reporting harmful content helps make the Internet safer and more enjoyable for everyone. If you're unsure whether something you see counts, but you feel it might, it's best to report it and let the platform decide.

What Is Harmful Content?

The term "harmful content" can cover a lot of things. Generally speaking, it's any content that could cause damage or distress. Harmful content might include things like:

- **Illegal activity:** Anything that breaks any laws or encourages breaking the law

- **Hate speech:** Using words to attack or talk badly about members of a particular group (like race, ethnicity, sexual orientation, or gender)

- **Discriminatory language:** Using words to exclude members of a particular group (race, ethnicity, sexual orientation, gender, and so on)

- **Images of violence or abuse:** Pictures or videos (real or created) that show violent or abusive behavior

- **Misinformation:** Any type of content that aims to distort or obscure the truth

- **Scam materials and malware:** Any content that tries to trick users into falling for scams or downloading computer viruses or other dangerous software

Your Digital Footprint — Think Before You Click

Everything we do online leaves a trace. That's not always a bad thing, but it is important to keep in mind when doing anything online.

WHAT IS A DIGITAL FOOTPRINT?

A digital footprint is a record of everything we do online — the sites we visit, the content we post, the comments we make — and much of it remains long after the feed moves on.

A digital footprint is like a tattoo. Once it's there, it's pretty much permanent. Trying to erase a tattoo is very difficult, and there are usually traces left behind. The same goes for a digital footprint — even if we remove the content, it can pop up unexpectedly.

There are two types of digital footprints:

- **Passive:** The cookies and trackers that collect as we move around the Internet.

- **Active:** The things we put out there voluntarily (or involuntarily) — messages, comments, videos, etc.

You control most of what you add to your active footprint — whatever you (or your friends) post online becomes part of it! You also have a fair amount of control over your passive footprint. In this section, we'll look at how to control both.

WHY SHOULD YOU CARE ABOUT YOUR DIGITAL FOOTPRINT?

Have you ever been absolutely certain about something, only to change your mind later on? Maybe you were a huge fan of a band when you were younger, but now you're not so keen on them (maybe they're even a bit embarrassing!). Or perhaps you once hated chocolate ice cream, but now it's your favorite.

It's a normal part of life to change your mind and opinions, and we all do things that we might later regret or feel embarrassed about. It's no different online. Things that we post can come back to haunt us!

Although you can "delete" a post from your social media accounts, it may still exist online — it just becomes invisible to you and other users, which is usually enough. But what if someone took a screenshot or shared the post before you deleted it? Then, you have no control over what happens with it.

Real-World Consequences of Online Behavior

Imagine you're online one evening, browsing TikTok and chatting with friends. A newcomer in your friend group points out a TikTok creator from your school that they dislike. They persuade everyone to leave silly comments on the creator's posts.

To you, the comments seem harmless and fun. Unfortunately, the creator doesn't feel that way and reports your whole group to TikTok and your school. You receive discipline at school, and the incident goes on your permanent record.

Years later, when you apply for college, your top choices reject you because of the blemish on your record. One thoughtless action can permanently impact your digital footprint and cause unintended consequences, even years later.

Of course, this is an extreme example of how poor online behavior can have unexpected and unpleasant consequences. However, the takeaway is to think before you act and consider how it might affect the "future you."

How to Manage Your Digital Footprint

To avoid your digital footprint causing problems, it's important to manage it mindfully. Here are three things to remember to help you keep on top of it.

1. Explore your privacy settings.

Every social media platform and website that you can log on to will have a privacy settings section. It might be called "preferences," "settings," or something else. When you find it, go through the settings and activate those that give you the most privacy. That means opting out of sharing information where possible, keeping viewers of your posts to contacts only, and not allowing people you don't know to comment/send messages. Check these settings regularly.

2. Think twice, post once.

Before you post anything online or even send a message, think carefully. Ask yourself, "Would I be okay with everyone seeing this?" If the answer is "no," it might be better not to post it.

3. Remember that once you've posted something, it's out of your control.

People can take screenshots and share your posts if they want to, so don't count on being able to post something and then delete it. Don't post it if you aren't happy with it being out there forever.

What to Share and What to Keep to Yourself

If you're unsure whether to post or share content online, consider what it contains. Some types of content are almost always safe, and others are nearly always a bad idea. Remember that sharing a post is the same as posting it — you align yourself with the content.

- **Safe**: Posts about your achievements and positive experiences, as long as they don't have any personal details like your address, school, or location. You can always use photo editing software to remove these details.

- **Not safe**: Anything showing personal details, like your address, school, or location; posts showing illegal or harmful activity, or other kinds of bad behavior; and private photographs of yourself or others.

REMEMBER!

Here's a good rule of thumb: **If you're unsure whether something is appropriate to post, don't post it!** You can always decide to share it later if you change your mind, but you can't take it back once it's out there.

What is Appropriate to Post?

To help decide if something is appropriate to post, ask yourself:

1. Who will see it?
2. Would I be comfortable if my parents, teachers, or friends saw it?
3. Does it reveal personal or others' information?
4. Could it hurt someone's feelings?
5. Would I be proud to show it to my future self?
6. What do I hope to achieve with this post?

Now, it's your turn: Think about what's safe and respectful to share and what's not.

Safe to Post...	Not Safe to Post...

Using Social Media Responsibly

Social media hasn't been around that long, but it plays a massive role in modern life. From the early days of IRC channels, MSN Messenger, and Angelfire web pages (ask your parents!) to chatrooms and Myspace, Facebook, WhatsApp, Snapchat, and TikTok, we live in the social media age.

What Is Social Media?

Social media is any online platform where users can create and share content with others. That content might be simple messages (WhatsApp, for example), multimedia posts (like Instagram), or short-form videos (as with TikTok).

Social media platforms use "algorithms" to decide what content to show individual users.

What Is an Algorithm?

An algorithm is a set of instructions that computers follow to solve problems or complete tasks.

Humans also use algorithms in our daily lives! Think about getting ready for school in the morning. Chances are, you get up, get dressed, and eat breakfast the same way each day. You can think of each step as a different algorithm in your "Getting Ready for School" program.

How Do Social Media Algorithms Work?

Have you noticed that if you look at something on social media — cute bunny videos, for example — more of that type of content comes up in your feed? That's a social media algorithm at work. You get shown more cute bunny videos because the algorithm thinks they're what you're into — and who doesn't want more of what they love, right?

A social media algorithm aims to keep you engaged — keeping you on the platform and interacting with content for as long as possible. It does this by tracking what you do on the platform (and often across other platforms) and how you engage with content. It notices what you stop scrolling to look at, what you scroll right past, what you "like," what you comment on, what you share...everything.

By tracking what you engage with, the algorithm works out how to keep you engaged and interacting on the platform. It's important to note that the algorithm doesn't know or care what you actually enjoy, what makes you happy or sad, or what is healthy. Its only aim is to keep you on the platform. As long as you interact with content, it's doing its job.

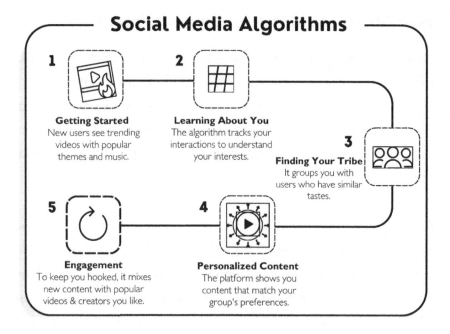

Social Media Algorithms

1 Getting Started
New users see trending videos with popular themes and music.

2 Learning About You
The algorithm tracks your interactions to understand your interests.

3 Finding Your Tribe
It groups you with users who have similar tastes.

4 Personalized Content
The platform shows you content that match your group's preferences.

5 Engagement
To keep you hooked, it mixes new content with popular videos & creators you like.

HOW MIGHT SOCIAL MEDIA ALGORITHMS CAUSE TROUBLE?

There is a lot of discussion about social media algorithms, their effects, and whether they are potentially dangerous. Let's explore some of the ways that social media algorithms might cause problems.

- **Creating echo chambers:** When people only see content that reflects their worldviews, they often forget that other people have different opposing ideas. This is particularly true when it comes to politics or elections.

- **Spreading misinformation:** Algorithms are computer programs that prioritize high-engagement sensationalist stories over true factual ones, resulting in the spreading of fake news.

- **Boosting harmful content:** As with misinformation, algorithms promote content that gets a lot of engagement. Social media algorithms may automatically promote dangerous, divisive, and extremist content that gains engagement.

- **Using addictive techniques:** These algorithms have been designed to keep people engaged and stop them from leaving. Personal recommendations, notifications, and autoplay features aim to keep you scrolling, and they're almost impossible to resist.

How to Manage Social Media Algorithms

Ultimately, social media companies decide what systems they use, and users don't have much control over that. However, users can control which platforms they use and how they respond to content.

It's difficult to control what social media algorithms show you completely. However, you can manage the situation in a few ways:

1. Use site/app settings and preferences to limit data collection and opt out of personalized advertising where possible.

2. Engage with content that you like rather than content that you dislike. Engaging with content you dislike only means seeing more of it.

3. Follow new accounts with content you want to see, and unfollow or block accounts with content you don't want to see.

4. If you start seeing content that makes you feel uncomfortable, reset your social media feeds. The process is different for each platform, so search for "reset [name of platform] algorithm" for each platform you'd like to clean up. It's a good idea to do this every six months or so.

Privacy Settings Check-Up

Review your privacy settings for every social media platform regularly to ensure they're as strong as possible. Opt out of personalized ads and data collection where possible. Ask a trusted adult for help if necessary.

What Does Responsible Social Media Use Look Like?

Using social media responsibly is simple. It means:

- Being mindful of the content you post, share, and engage with

- Using privacy settings to keep yourself safe

- Interacting with others respectfully and safely

Thinking Before Posting

Remember that everything you say and do online can affect you and others. Sometimes, these consequences might happen immediately, but other times, they might come up years after the original post. Your words have weight.

What you say online impacts others, often in ways you might not intend. Online communication can easily lead to misunderstandings, so that joke you think is funny might not be well received by everyone.

Think about how it would make you feel to see something negative about you or one of your friends. It would hurt, right? Even a joke can be hurtful, whether the teller intended it that way or not.

A responsible social media user aims to uplift others rather than bring them down. Consider posting positive content that brightens someone's day instead of negative things that might upset people.

The Pause Principle

Before you post anything, pause and ask yourself, "Is this something I'd be okay with everyone seeing, even years in the future?" If the answer is "no," it's probably a good idea to hold off. The future you will thank you!

Your posts might be seen by future colleges, employers, and others, so it's important to post things that reflect positively on you.

UNDERSTANDING ONLINE VS. OFFLINE RELATIONSHIPS

It's common for people to have friends that they met online, and who they may never meet in the offline world. Online friendships are not necessarily bad but come with an extra layer of uncertainty. The possibility of being deceived is real, and it's much harder to judge people's intentions online than offline.

It is vitally important to keep your wits about you when making online friends. Anonymity and the potential for people to lie about their identity mean that not everyone is who they say they are or has your best interests at heart.

Friend or Faux?

Sometimes, a person might pretend to be your friend for their own reasons. This can happen offline and online, but it's harder to spot on the internet — especially if you don't know what warning signs to look for. Some red flags that might suggest someone isn't who they claim to be include:

- **Suspicious behavior:** The person avoids voice or video calls and doesn't provide additional photos to prove their identity.

- **Unrealistic profile:** Their social media profile seems too "perfect" or too good to be true.

- **Pressure tactics:** They may press you to give personal information, send pictures, or do things you don't want to do.

- **Inconsistent information:** The details they give about themselves don't line up, or they frequently change their story.

- **Fake photos:** They refuse to show their real face, instead using stock images, AI-generated photos, or other people's photos. You can use Google image search to check the authenticity of their photos.

These are not necessarily signs that a person is lying about their identity, but they're indicators that they may not have your best interests at heart. Don't be afraid to set boundaries about when and what you want to discuss. A real friend won't push you into giving information or try to get you to do things you don't want to.

If you feel uncomfortable in an online conversation, whether with someone you've just met or a person you've known for a while, it's important to tell a trusted adult.

Influencer Real Talk

Do you have any favorite TikTok, Instagram, or YouTube creators? Chances are, you follow at least a few people who make content about something you're interested in. Whether it's pop music, makeup, wrestling, mountain biking, or reading, there's content out there for every passion.

What Is an Influencer?

An influencer is someone who creates content on social media that appeals to specific audiences or focuses on particular topics. These individuals earn money by gaining followers and partnering with companies to promote products. A well-known example is MrBeast, who began posting videos on YouTube in 2012 and now has hundreds of millions of subscribers.

Influencers are not new — people have been influencing each other for a long time. However, social media influencers are unique in that they can connect with people across the globe.

While it may appear simple, being a successful influencer involves significant effort and consistency in producing engaging content.

Many influencers only share the best parts of their lives, making it seem like they live perfectly, without any troubles. This isn't the whole truth. They often show a "perfect" version that's carefully crafted for their audience, as this is part of their job.

While it can be fun to see someone engaging in exciting activities, remember they experience the same frustrations and challenges as everyone else — they just don't share those bits online. This selective sharing of "perfection" can sometimes make us feel like our own lives are lacking or don't measure up in comparison. It's important to remember that what we see is not always the complete picture.

SETTING UP A SOCIAL MEDIA PROFILE SAFELY

Social media is an easy and fun way to keep in touch with friends and family and meet new friends. But it's important to set up your profiles safely and securely. Don't worry — it's simple when you know how!

How to Create a Safe and Engaging Profile

Your Screen Name

Be creative: Choose something related to your interests and hobbies, your pet's name, or something you love.

Don't get personal: Avoid using too much personal information, like your full name, location, or school.

Your Profile Picture

Use a picture that you find fun and expressive, but doesn't give away any personal information. It's okay to show your face, but avoid including anything that shows where you live or go to school. Always double-check the background of your photo to ensure it doesn't give away too much information.

Your Content

Before you post or share anything online, think carefully about whether it's a good idea. If you decide to go for it, ensure no personal details are visible in the post. Feel free to share information about what you love and enjoy doing, but don't share anything that could reveal where you live or go to school.

Social Media Dos and Don'ts

Do:

- Get to know the privacy settings and check them regularly.

- Use different strong passwords for all your accounts.

- Think before you post, comment, or share.

- Be selective about who you talk to.

- Be kind and respectful.

- Report any inappropriate or harmful content.

Don't:

- Share personal information.

- Share your passwords.

- Meet people offline.

- Accept requests or respond to messages from people you don't know.

- Be a troll or a bully.

- Pretend to be someone else.

- Get drawn into online arguments.

Managing Interactions

Adjust your privacy settings to prevent messages from people you don't know, if possible. This helps protect you from potential predators posing as friends.

If this isn't an option, be cautious when responding to messages or accepting friend requests from strangers. Remember, you don't have to respond to every request. Your safety is more important than what a stranger thinks of you.

If you receive messages from anyone — known or unknown — that make you feel uncomfortable or concerned, report them and tell a trusted adult.

COMMUNICATING IN A DIGITAL WORLD: HOW TO INTERACT EFFECTIVELY ONLINE

What's the one thing that all living things have in common? You might have heard of the seven common characteristics of living organisms — movement, respiration, sensitivity, growth, reproduction, excretion, and nutrition — but something else ties us all together, from tiny ants to humans: **Communication.**

The Evolution of Communication

Humans have developed incredible ways to communicate over hundreds of thousands of years. But the communication we take for granted today, like speaking on a phone or messaging friends, is just a recent development. Let's take a look back and see how communication has changed over the years.

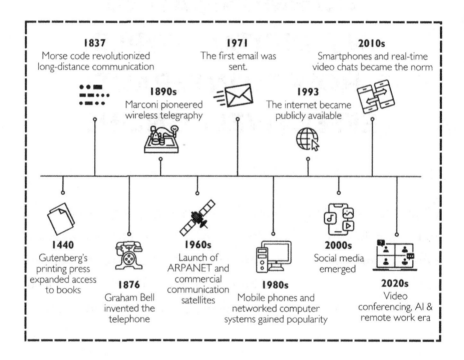

What Is Communication?

Simply put, it's the passing of information from one organism to another — and there are many different ways to do it. From speaking, dancing, howling, and growling to changing color or wafting chemical signals through the air, the world around us buzzes with creatures of all kinds sending messages!

THE DIGITAL REVOLUTION

As you can see from the timeline, communication technology made massive strides between the 19th and 21st centuries. In just over 200 years, humans went from sending messages via carrier pigeons to instant messaging and Zoom calls!

This leap began with the discovery and application of radio waves in the late 1800s. People realized that detailed information could be sent and received almost instantly over long distances, setting the stage for the instant information culture of the present day.

With each new development in the communication timeline, people had to learn new skills. When the telephone was introduced, that meant learning how to make and receive calls. This might seem simple today, but imagine if you'd never seen a phone before.

Fast-forward to today, and there are many more communication technologies to learn.

When the telephone was invented, there was much discussion about how to answer when picking up the phone and how to end the call. To us, saying "Hello" and "Goodbye" seems obvious, but back then, people were still working it out.

Alexander Graham Bell, the inventor of the telephone, thought a jolly "Ahoy!" would work best as a greeting, while others favored "Speak." Pretty quickly, "Hello" became the most popular choice.

Early phone books recommended saying, "That is all," and hanging up to end the conversation. Maybe people thought it seemed rude or abrupt, but "Goodbye" won out.

Mastering Email

Communication is fundamental to modern life, and it's constantly evolving. That means it's a great idea to continually improve your communication skills!

With that in mind, let's look at some common communication technologies. Although you might not need to use all of these daily, having the skills is helpful, as you never know when you might need them.

Email has existed for more than 50 years, going from a novelty to a basic form of communication. Today, many (although certainly not all) people use email for work, business, or other "official" purposes.

EMAIL WRITING

Writing an email is like writing a letter (ask your grandparents!). Just like letter writing, there are accepted ways to email correctly. Because emails are often sent in a work environment, the tone tends to be quite formal, although they're usually a little more laid-back than a letter. Most of the time, the person sending the email knows the receiver but may not be close friends.

When writing an email, the first thing to consider is what you are trying to say. Then, think about who you are saying it to. These two things will help you choose the best tone, greeting, and sign-off.

What Is "Professional" or Formal Language?

You'll see this term a lot. It's best to use professional language whenever you talk or type with someone you know in a formal context, like a school teacher, a college professor, a colleague, or an employer. This means being clear and to the point, using proper spelling and grammar, and avoiding slang.

CRAFTING THE PERFECT EMAIL

Writing a good email that effectively conveys your message is pretty simple when you break it down into a few key components. The trick is to keep it clear and to the point.

- **Subject:** This short sentence summarizes what the email is about. For example, "Question about Spanish homework."

- **Greeting:** Start with a polite greeting. The exact wording depends on who will read the email (the recipient) and how well you know them.

Unless you know the recipient very well, it's best to use a formal greeting like "Dear [name]," including any titles like "Dr." or "Professor." If you're unsure, It's usually better to be too formal rather than too informal.

If you're writing to a close friend, you'll probably start with "Hi [name]," "Hello," or just their name.

- **Body:** This is where your message goes. Aim to keep it short, while still providing all the relevant details. Be careful not to ramble! Organize your points clearly so they're easy to read and understand. The following format works well:

  1. Start with your main point or question.

  2. Explain why it's important.

  3. Add any other necessary details.

- **Sign-off:** The sign-off wraps up your email. The way you sign off should match the tone of your email and your relationship with the recipient. For someone you don't know well, stick to formal sign-offs, like "Yours faithfully," "Respectfully," or "Best regards." For people you know in a formal setting, such as teachers, "Sincerely" or "Thanks" works well.

For emails to friends, family, or other people you're close to, you can use a more relaxed expression, like "Bye for now," "See you soon," or "Have a great weekend."

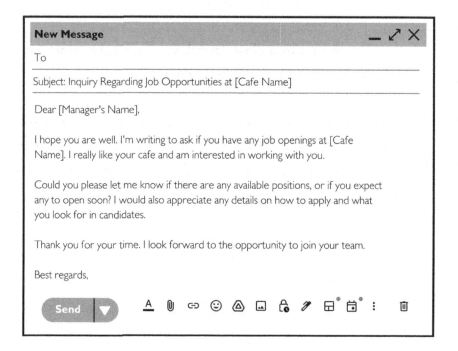

Replying Options

CC and BCC: When replying to or sending emails, you'll see the options "CC" and "BCC." Most of the time, you can ignore these options, but here's what they stand for:

- "CC" is short for "carbon copy," you use it if you want to send a copy of your email to another person to keep them in the loop. Using CC signals that the person copied in doesn't need to respond. With CC, everyone in the email chain can see the email addresses of those to whom the email has been sent and those who have been copied in.

- "BCC" stands for "blind carbon copy." It works like CC, except the email address of the person copied in is hidden.

Reply all: To reply to an email, just hit "Reply," type your message, and send. Sometimes, though, if you receive an email from a group and want to share your response with everyone, you can "Reply all." This sends your message to all the original recipients, including those who have been CC'd.

MANAGING YOUR INBOX

A disorganized inbox has become a joke among almost everyone with an email address. With potentially hundreds or even thousands of emails pouring in daily, keeping an inbox tidy can be a real challenge. But that doesn't mean you have to give in to a messy inbox! Using a few tricks makes it easy to keep your inbox organized.

1. **Unsubscribe:** Avoid signing up for email subscriptions. If you receive promotional emails you're no longer interested in, look for an "unsubscribe" link. This is usually at the bottom of the email.

2. **Delete:** Delete emails you don't need as soon as possible to stop them from piling up in your inbox.

3. **Search:** If you need to find a particular email, search for it rather than scrolling through your inbox.

4. **Use folders and labels:** Choose ways to categorize emails and make folders and labels so you can find them quickly and easily. Categories might include particular projects, friend groups, or interests. You can set categories and labels in the settings area of your inbox.

5. **Set filters:** Email filters can automatically sort incoming emails into their relevant folders based on the sender, subject, or keywords you set. Look in the settings section of your inbox to set filters. Your email provider will already use a spam filter, which you can manually change in the settings.

6. **Embrace the archive:** Use the archive function to keep important emails without cluttering your inbox.

7. **Do regular inbox maintenance:** Set aside time each day or week to go through your inbox, organize emails, respond to messages, and clear out clutter.

8. **Limit your notifications:** Reduce email notifications (or even turn them off) so you're not constantly interrupted by incoming emails. Instead, check your inbox at regular times.

9. **Respond promptly:** Respond to emails immediately so the unanswered ones don't pile up in your inbox.

Handling Spam and Phishing

Some emails that find their way into your inbox will be spam or phishing attempts. At best, these emails are a waste of time and space. At worst, they're dangerous.

What Is Spam?

"Spam" is any unwanted or excessive electronic communication. It's those emails you get three times a day from a website you visited once, and the constant stream of emojis your friend puts in your group chat. Spam is annoying but usually harmless. However, it can sometimes be dangerous. It might contain links to harmful downloads or phishing attempts.

HOW TO DEAL WITH SPAM

- **Use a spam filter:** The best way to deal with spam is to use a good email filter. Most email providers already have one set up, and you can tweak it to your liking in the settings.

- **Avoid opening spam emails:** If an email looks suspicious, don't open it.

- **Mark messages as spam:** If a spam email gets through to your inbox, mark it as spam. This will help your spam filter become more effective.

HOW TO RECOGNIZE A PHISHING ATTEMPT

"Phishing" is when a scammer tries to trick you into giving away sensitive or personal information. The goal is to gather enough information to get into your accounts, usually to steal money.

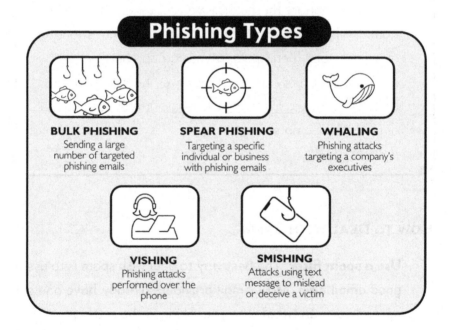

Phishing Types

BULK PHISHING
Sending a large number of targeted phishing emails

SPEAR PHISHING
Targeting a specific individual or business with phishing emails

WHALING
Phishing attacks targeting a company's executives

VISHING
Phishing attacks performed over the phone

SMISHING
Attacks using text message to mislead or deceive a victim

Phishing attempts can be very sophisticated and hard to spot. It's best to treat any email or message that asks you to log into an account or send details as suspicious. If in doubt, do not follow any instructions. Check online for similar scam messages.

PayPal, Amazon, Facebook, and other such accounts are prime targets for phishing scammers. Never follow links from emails. Instead, type in the proper URL address yourself. Banks will never ask you to send information by message or email.

Be wary of messages telling you you've won a prize or have a limited time to respond. These are almost always phishing or other scam attempts. Scammers often try to invoke a sense of urgency or panic in their victims so that they won't stop and think. Scammers do this because it works — so always take time to think about what you're doing.

Video Conferencing

It's very common these days to use video conferencing instead of face-to-face meetings. Faster Internet speeds and improved video technology have made these tools accessible at home. The COVID-19 pandemic accelerated this trend and made working and schooling from home a necessity. While face-to-face interaction is back in many areas, the ease of video conferencing means it's here to stay.

How to Video Conference Like a Pro

Video conferencing is quite simple when you get the hang of it. The best way to ensure that things run smoothly is to set up your equipment and space before the call. Here are a few pointers to help you.

1. **Set up in a quiet spot:** Choose a quiet area with minimal background noise and distractions. Ensure other people know not to disturb you while on the call. Keep pets out of the room, unless you know they'll be welcome on the call.

2. **Dress appropriately:** You might be at home, but that doesn't mean video conferencing in your pajamas is a good idea. Wear clothes that you would wear if you were attending the meeting offline to give a good impression and help you feel prepared.

3. **Arrange your camera:** Set up your space so that you appear face-on in the middle of the screen. Aim to appear one or two feet from the camera — not too close or too far away. You can check how your setup looks in the video settings of your conferencing software.

4. **Choose your background:** Use an area with as little going on in the background as possible to avoid distracting other participants. A neutral wall is ideal. Avoid using novelty in-app backgrounds unless you're talking with your friends, as they can give the wrong impression. Make sure no personal details are visible in your background.

5. **Fix the lighting:** Choose a well-lit area, ideally with two or three light sources in different places. Try to ensure that you are evenly lit and that there are no dark shadows. Close the curtains or blinds if too much light comes in through a window.

6. **Use headphones:** Headphones can help you to concentrate on the conversation and avoid distractions. They also improve the audio quality and help to reduce background noise. Make sure your headphones have a built-in microphone.

7. **Test your tech:** Before the meeting, check that your Internet connection, webcam, microphone, and necessary software are working. Also, test your audio and video settings — look in your video conferencing software's "Settings" or "Preferences" section. Give yourself enough time to tackle any problems — half an hour should do it.

Video Conferencing Etiquette

Once you're set up, it's time for the call. Follow these tips to make a great impression.

Videocon Etiquette

BE ON TIME
Log into the meeting two to five minutes early.

PARTICIPATE ACTIVELY
Ask and answer questions, and stay engaged.

PRACTICE EYE CONTACT
Look directly into the camera when you talk.

MUTE YOUR MICROPHONE
Ask and answer questions, and stay engaged.

MINIMIZE DISTRACTONS
Close unnecessary tabs and silence notifications and alerts.

FOLLOW MEETING ETIQUETTE
Wait your turn to speak, do not interrupt, and use polite language.

Phone Etiquette

The term "smartphone" is a bit misleading. Yes, smartphones make calls. But is that what people use them for most of the time? Probably not. Most of us use them for messaging, browsing the Internet, social media, and shopping more than for actual phone calls.

Interestingly, a surprising number of people struggle with speaking on the phone. Maybe it's because we're so used to texting or using video calls, where the rules and social cues are a little different.

How to Make and Receive Phone Calls

The good news is that, by being prepared (and with a little bit of practice), it's easy to develop phone skills.

1. **Make a plan:** Before the call, note down the points you want to make or questions you want to ask.

2. **Pick your time:** Aim to call when the other person is likely available and happy to talk. Check their time zone and call according to theirs, not yours. If it's 5 pm for you but 1 am for them, it's better to call earlier in the day!

3. **Say hi/introduce yourself:** If you know the person you're calling, start the call by saying, "Hello, it's [your name]. How are you?" If you don't know them, go with, "Hello, my name is [your name], and I'm calling about [your reason for calling]."

4. **Be polite:** Use polite language and a friendly tone throughout the conversation. Respect the other person's time and avoid interrupting them while they speak.

5. **Pay attention:** Listen carefully to what the other person is saying. If it's an important call, take notes to remember what was said.

6. **Speak clearly:** It can be harder to understand what people are saying on the phone, as there are no visual clues. Make sure to speak at your normal speed and volume, and keep the microphone near your mouth.

7. **Stay focused:** Try to stay on topic. If you notice the call going off track, gently guide it back on topic.

8. **Be careful with information:** Don't publicly discuss sensitive or confidential information (your own or other people's) where others might overhear.

9. **Sign-off politely:** Thank the other person for their time and make any plans for follow-up actions or calls. Finish with a friendly "Bye!"

Online Messaging

Texting and online messaging are great ways to stay in touch, regardless of the apps you use. But as with every form of communication, there are good and not-so-good ways to use them.

Texting Done Right

Everyone has their texting style and preferences, and it's OK to text however you like. That said, there are a few things to bear in mind.

Using Emojis

It can be quite difficult to convey exactly what you mean when texting, especially if you're making a joke or writing something that could be interpreted in different ways. That's what emojis are for! Emojis are a great way to ensure your meaning is understood — if you use them right.

Emojis are best used in casual situations, like messaging with friends. Avoid using them too much, unless you know that the person you're texting with likes to use them a lot, as some people find them annoying. Also, bear in mind that many emojis have specific meanings. If you want to use a particular emoji and aren't sure what it means, look it up online first.

Responding Mindfully

When texting, sometimes you chat back and forth quickly, and other times, there might be longer breaks between messages. Some people reply immediately and are happy with a constant stream of messages, while others prefer to respond at a time that suits them better.

There's no right or wrong way to text, but respecting the other person's time and preferences is essential. Don't expect an immediate reply all the time. Sometimes, people are too busy to respond or need time to think about what you've said. At the same time, don't leave someone hanging "on read" for too long, or they may feel you're ignoring them.

When to Call Instead

If you need to discuss something urgent or confidential — or feel you are in danger — it's best to call instead of texting.

Group Chats

Group chats are a fun way to chat with a bunch of friends. They're great for sharing jokes or sorting out plans for hanging out, but they're not the right choice for every situation.

Group chats are best for lighthearted conversations or for planning specific events. If you need to discuss something you'd rather not have everyone in the chat know about, use direct messaging instead. It's also important to be mindful of other people's privacy.

Group Chat Behavior

DO	DON'T
• **Use Appropriate Language:** Help everyone feel comfortable.	• **Don't Invite Strangers:** Keep group chats for friends, family, and known people.
• **Be Respectful:** Treat everyone with kindness.	• **Don't Spam:** Avoid sending lots of messages, emojis, or stickers at once.
• **Include Everyone:** Avoid private jokes and exclusion.	• **Don't Argue:** Disagree calmly and respectfully.
• **Think Before You Send:** Pause and consider before posting.	• **Don't Be Afraid to Leave:** Exit the group if you feel uncomfortable or need a break.
• **Follow the Rules:** Read and adhere to them.	• **Don't Be a Cyberbully:** Avoid excluding people, being nasty, and name-calling.
• **Set Boundaries:** Mute notifications during specified times.	• **Don't Spread Gossip:** Avoid talking behind others' backs or sharing screenshots.
• **Report Issues:** Report mean or inappropriate content.	• **Don't Share Personal Info:** Never share addresses, phone numbers, or passwords in an open group chat.

Empathy in the Digital Age

Digital communication can sometimes feel a little "soulless." It can be easy to forget that the people we're talking to are people with feelings, just like us. Offline, it's easier to see whether a person is laughing, smiling, or crying, which helps us decide what to do or say next. Understanding how our actions affect others online can be a lot harder.

BEING THERE WITHOUT BEING THERE

If someone you know is struggling, it's important to be there and help them. Our lives and relationships are strengthened and richer when we do this for each other. But what about if you're not physically in the same place?

It's still possible to be there when you're not there. Sometimes, people even find opening up to be easier with a little physical distance. Supporting a friend online is not so different from helping them offline — it comes down to listening. Here are a few tips on how to be a supportive friend. They'll work wherever you are (or aren't!).

1. **Listen actively:** Pay full attention to what the other person is saying, and don't interrupt. Don't check your phone or do other things on your computer. Show your friends you're listening to them by making eye contact — look into the camera.

2. **Show understanding:** Acknowledge what your friend says as their truth, even if you see things differently. Don't argue with them about what they're experiencing or feeling.

3. **Don't judge:** Avoid giving your opinions or advice unless your friend asks.

4. **Let them know they're not alone:** Even if you're on different sides of the world, make sure they know you're there for them.

5. **Respect their boundaries:** Sometimes people don't want to talk, and that's OK. Don't press them, but let them know you're there when they are ready. Then, offer to do something else together instead, like playing a game.

6. **Check in**: Don't wait for your friend to get in touch. Let them know you're there by dropping them a message or voice note now and again and arranging calls or hangouts with them.

LOOKING AFTER YOURSELF

Although it's important to be there for the people around us, both online and offline, we also need to look after our mental health. Sometimes, supporting others can be too much. If you feel overwhelmed or can't give a friend the support they need, respectfully tell them.

WHEN TO GET HELP

If your friend tells you they're being bullied, threatened, or made to feel unsafe, encourage them to get help from a trusted adult. Don't be afraid to tell a trusted adult yourself if necessary.

5

FINDING AND HANDLING INFORMATION: SMART STRATEGIES FOR THE DIGITAL AGE

The Internet is like a massive digital library where the answers to all your questions are just a few clicks or taps away. While that's pretty awesome, it's very easy to get lost! There is a lot of irrelevant stuff in the world's biggest library, so finding your way is an important skill.

The Internet — Your Digital Library

The Internet puts a world of information at your fingertips. People have unlimited access to information and knowledge for the first time in history, without leaving the comfort of their homes.

It's a powerful resource, but, as you probably know, "with great power comes great responsibility." Learning to navigate the online world is essential to thrive in it.

MASTERING WEB SEARCHES

Just like in a library, you need to know what you're looking for and how to find it to find what you want online. That means perfecting the art of the search query or search term.

There are many ways to ensure you get valuable results when searching online. Here are a few tips to help you get the most out of your searches.

1. **Use a reputable search engine.** Google is the most commonly used, but other options exist, such as DuckDuckGo and Bing.

2. **Use specific keywords:** Try to be as specific as possible. For example, if you're looking for information on Marvel comics from between 1980 and 1990, search for "Marvel comics between 1980 and 1990" rather than just "Marvel comics." The more you narrow it down, the better your results will be.

3. **Use quotation marks:** Quotation marks help you search for exact phrases. Using "" around your search phrase will search for those exact words in that order, so you'll get better results.

4. **Use filters:** Search engine filters let you narrow down results by date, location, and content type to find more relevant information.

5. **Use advanced search operators**: If you want to get super specific, try some advanced search operators. Here are a few examples:

   a. **"–" (Minus sign):** Use this to exclude terms you don't want in your search results. For instance, if you type "Marvel comics–Spider-Man," you'll get results for Marvel comics without much about Spider-Man.

   b. **"OR"**: This lets you search for one thing or another. So, if you're unsure, you can look up "Spider-Man OR Batman" to find information on both.

   c. **"define:"**: If you want to know what a word means, use "define:" followed by the word, and you'll get its definition.

   To discover more advanced search commands, search [advanced search commands] on your favorite search engine!

6. **Check the search suggestions:** As you type your query, look at the autocomplete search suggestions. You might see the exact phrase you're looking for, or notice something you hadn't thought of.

7. **Search by voice:** Most search engines allow you to search using your voice, which can be faster than typing and more convenient if you're out and about.

8. **Image search:** Your searches don't have to be text-based. You can also upload an image or image URL. This can be handy when seeking information on a particular item, place, or person.

Understanding Search Results

Once you've got your search results, you need to know how to interpret them. You'll get a few different kinds of results, and some are more useful than others.

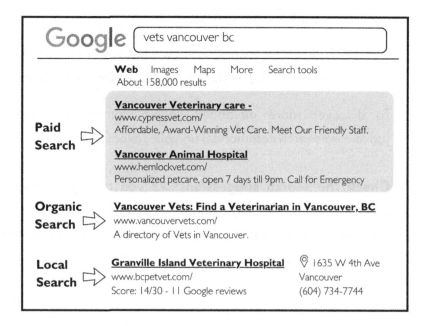

Sponsored Results

Sponsored listings usually appear at the top of the results page and are often marked as "sponsored." This means someone has paid the search engine to show their site or product, hoping to get more visitors. When you click on a sponsored listing, the advertiser usually pays the search engine a small fee for bringing you to their site.

While sponsored results are not necessarily bad, it's important to note that not all sponsored listings are trustworthy. Scammers often create fake sites and have them sponsored to trick people into visiting them, so watch out.

Organic Results

These are the results that have not been paid for. Their order is based on how well the search algorithm thinks they fit your search term and how much value they provide. The closer a website is to what you're looking for, the higher you should see them in the results.

Assessing Website Credibility

Not all websites are trustworthy. Even if a site looks slick and professional, there may be reasons to doubt its credibility. Learning to determine whether a website (or a newspaper, book, or any other source online or offline) is credible is crucial.

What Is Credibility?

Credibility means being trustworthy and reliable. It's usually earned over a long period of time by telling the truth and acting without underhanded or shady motives. People build credibility by working hard and honestly within their fields of expertise, and publications (newspapers, news sites, and so on) build credibility by behaving truthfully and honorably. Lying, cheating, and being deceptive are easy ways to lose credibility.

How to Assess Credibility Online

Don't believe everything you read. When you're online, keeping your critical thinking cap on is crucial! Use these tips to help you understand whether something you see online is trustworthy.

1. **Consider the content:** Look at the content closely. Check for errors and mistakes, or things that seem "off." Does the content seem one-sided, or is it trying to get you to take a particular view? Are there any experts or reputable organizations involved, or any citations? Is the language trying to provoke anger or negativity toward a specific group?

2. **Check the sources:** Look at where the information comes from, who made it, and when. Sometimes, people use their platforms to cause trouble or push an agenda, even if they pretend otherwise. Information from trusted sources, such as educational institutions, government websites, and reputable news outlets, is generally trustworthy. Blogs, TikTok videos, and social media posts are often personal opinions — that doesn't make them wrong, but they should not automatically be treated as fact.

3. **Look for signs of trustworthiness:** A professionally made website isn't automatically trustworthy, but it is something to look for. Other things to look for include people using their real names for their content, quotes, references, citations from trusted organizations, and honesty about the site's goals and funding.

4. **Check the domain:** Websites with domains (the bit in the address after the ".") like .gov (government websites) and .edu (educational institutions) are generally more credible than those with generic domains like .com or .biz.

Spotting Fake News and Bias

Having such easy access to information has a lot of advantages, and it's great that people today can have their perspectives heard by millions of others around the world. However, not everything that ends up online should be taken as fact.

Some people have particular reasons for promoting certain ideas, some like telling lies, and some want to cause trouble. Other times, the truth at the center of the story is spun into something completely different.

What Is Bias?

In this context, "bias" means treating a particular person or group more favorably or worse than another. A bias favoring a group means treating them better, and a bias against a group means treating them worse. Biases are not always obvious and can exist deep in society and people's behavior.

How to Identify Fake News and Bias

It's vital to learn how to distinguish between reliable information, information that could be suspect, and false information. It's not always easy, but some reliable techniques will help you. These tips build on the methods mentioned above for determining whether a source is credible. Always use those as a baseline.

1. **Use your critical thinking skills:** Being able to tell the difference between fact, opinion, and lies is vital to thriving both online and offline. Consider why information may be

presented the way it is and keep your mind open to different perspectives.

2. **Read the headline:** Headlines are supposed to attract attention, but if they use wildly exaggerated language, make wild claims, or use all caps or exclamation marks, there's a good chance they're not to be trusted.

3. **Check for supporting sources:** Real news will have reliable sources to support its claims. Look for links to scientific studies and quotes from experts and research them. Quotes and studies can be misrepresented, so it's important to look at the original source.

4. **Don't believe everything you see:** Images and videos are easy to manipulate. Always check the sources of images and videos, and be wary if no source is given or the source lacks credibility. You can use reverse image search to check where else images have appeared online.

5. **Check the date:** Sometimes, people present old news as recent. Always check the date of a story or piece of content and consider why someone might want to present it as more recent than it is.

6. **Always fact check:** Go through the content for anything presented as a fact and check it against other trusted sources, like government or educational institution websites. The more cross-checking with other sources you do, the better. Check

that the author or creator of the content is who they say they are, and that they are being honest about their credentials. Use reliable fact-checking websites like Snopes.com to investigate claims.

THE LURE OF CLICKBAIT

With so much content vying for Internet users' attention, "clickbait" has become a common way to get views. Unfortunately, as an Internet user, it's often a waste of time.

What Is Clickbait?

Clickbait is unremarkable content with a sensational title or thumbnail (often both). The idea is that the title and thumbnail are so irresistible to anyone who sees them that they just have to click and view the content. Usually, the content is not nearly as interesting as it pretends to be.

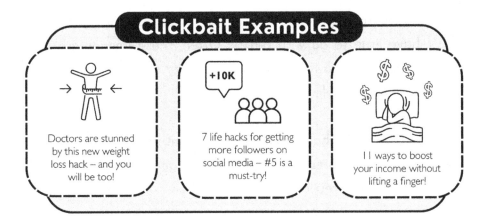

Clickbait Examples

Doctors are stunned by this new weight loss hack – and you will be too!

7 life hacks for getting more followers on social media – #5 is a must-try!

11 ways to boost your income without lifting a finger!

RECOGNIZING CLICKBAIT

Clickbait uses a few tricks to grab your attention. Here are some ways to spot it:

- **Angry headlines:** Sometimes, headlines are written to provoke anger or disbelief without telling the reader the story. For example, "You Won't Believe What This Terrible Person Did!"

- **Secrets and gossip:** If you see something like "Discover This One Trick to Reveal the Secret to Eternal Life!" it's probably clickbait. They promise big secrets, famous people doing incredible things, or discoveries to get you to click.

- **Question headlines:** Headlines that ask unrealistic or remarkable questions and often don't have great answers are usually clickbait. For example: "Do You Know This One Secret to Winning Fortnite?" sounds great, but unfortunately, it likely won't have the great answer it promises.

- **Eye-catching images:** Clickbait often uses images that have little to do with reality. Often, these images are AI-generated, showing celebrities in crazy situations or people doing impossible things.

Being able to tell what is clickbait from what isn't helps you avoid wasting time on content that's just trying to get you to click without offering anything real or valuable.

Navigating the World of AI

AI has been in the news in recent years. AI technology is playing an increasing role in many aspects of life, and this trend will likely continue. Learning how to understand this technology and make it work for you will be vitally important in the coming years.

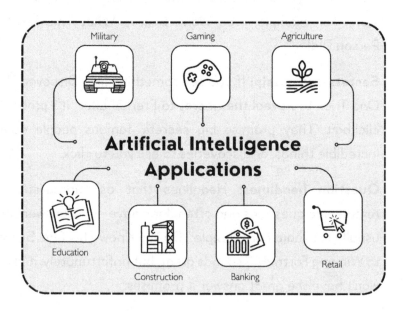

What Is AI?

"AI" stands for artificial intelligence. It is software designed to process information and "think" like a human, only faster. The term has been around since the mid-20th century, but technology has only recently caught up to the name.

Modern AI technologies combine, compare, and reshape existing information into new forms. This could involve working with huge amounts of data from deep space to construct models of the universe, or creating new images by processing every image on the Internet. Machine learning is the process whereby AI learns from the data we feed it.

AI can work with huge amounts of data much faster than humans, and can perform many "human-like" tasks, like spotting patterns and categorizing objects. At the moment, though, AI technology can't have ideas or think new thoughts — it can only work with what we feed it. In the future, that might change!

How to Prompt AI Effectively

Interacting with AI systems can be a lot of fun and make things like planning and researching faster and simpler than ever before. But to get the best results, you must know how to prompt.

What Is Prompting?

A prompt is a specific type of text you provide to an AI system, like a chatbot or an image generator, to produce the content you're looking for. The prompt guides the AI tool in generating the correct response.

---

1. **Be specific:** The more specific you are, the more likely you'll get the AI's output to match your expectations. For instance, instead of saying, "Show me a green field full of cows," try, "Show me a large, lush, green field with a herd of 17 longhorn cows, with mountains in the distance, under a clear sky as the sun sets." This level of detail helps the AI tool visualize exactly what you want.

2. **Give examples:** Include examples that closely match what you're looking for. For instance, for the "cows in a field" example, you might provide photos of the specific type of cows or the mountains you're looking for. This helps the AI tool understand the style you're seeking.

3. **Try different formats**: Experiment with questions, statements, and instructions to see how they affect the results. For instance, "How many people have been to the moon?" might prompt a chatty, informal response. "List all the people who have been to the moon" will likely prompt a simple list. Experimentation is key!

4. **Break it down:** Tackling large or complex tasks in parts rather than all at once is more effective. For instance, if you're asking an AI to produce a detailed image, focus on one part at a time — cows, then fields, then mountains, then sky. Once you're happy with each part, instruct the AI to combine them into one image.

5. **Build on results:** If the output isn't what you want, use it as a stepping stone for the next prompt. For instance, if the AI produces an image of a small brown cow with short horns, your next prompt might be, "Make the cow bigger and the horns two feet long." The AI model uses your prompts to understand and improve its outputs.

6. **Be realistic:** Remember that AI technology cannot think or create anything for itself. It operates with the information it has been trained on. In other words, don't expect it to come up with anything startlingly original! Use AI tools to enhance your work and productivity rather than relying on them to do all the work.

The Accuracy of AI

Although AI technology is impressive, it isn't perfect and can make mistakes. If you're using a system like ChatGPT or Bard, don't take what it says as fact. These systems are trained on billions of pieces of information, and not all of it is true. The AI doesn't know the difference, so it's up to you to check.

The AI's results might be outdated, error-ridden, or completely wrong. When an AI system produces false results, we call it "hallucinating."

AI, Plagiarism, and Copying

Remembering that AI does not generate original ideas or create new concepts is crucial. It is brilliant at rearranging information, but, unlike humans, it cannot create its own novel content.

A human has produced every piece of data that goes into an AI system, so although the output may be unique, it is never original. For this reason, it's important not to use AI to generate anything that is supposed to be your own work, such as schoolwork or exam answers. Generating work with AI and submitting it as your own is dishonest and could get you into big trouble.

> **What Is Plagiarism?**
>
> Plagiarism means taking someone else's work and pretending it's your own. It can be anything from copying an essay found online to taking quotations from a book without crediting the author. Plagiarism is very serious and can lead to getting in trouble in school, losing your credibility, and even being prosecuted.

Understanding Ownership and Copyright

Online, it's easy to access pretty much any kind of media content you like. Movies, games, music — it's all out there. To ensure that the people who create the content are treated fairly and paid for their work, we have laws in place about how we can get content, and how we can use it.

INTELLECTUAL PROPERTY, COPYRIGHT, AND YOU

When a person creates something, whether it's a film, book, piece of music, or one of the many other kinds of creations, that work is that person's intellectual property. This means they have legal rights to it. Intellectual property is protected by law, and stealing or using someone else's intellectual property without permission is illegal.

The rules that cover intellectual property are called copyrights. By creating something original, a person automatically has a copyright — they don't need to register the creation with anyone. If someone takes that work and pretends it's theirs without permission, that breaks copyright laws. So, if you write a story and someone else takes it and publishes it as their own, they're breaking the law!

Fair Use

One exception to copyright is "fair use." This is where someone uses a small part of a copyrighted work in a way that doesn't negatively affect the original work. In these cases, there is no need to get permission. Generally, it's best to get permission from the copyright holder and credit them if you use their work.

Where to Find Content

The Internet is full of places to find content legally. For music, there's Spotify, YouTube, Apple Music, and many other sources. Films are available from Netflix, Amazon, and many other providers. Steam is a great place to find games, and you can buy books from online booksellers like Amazon.

These platforms ensure that creators receive payment for their work and are acknowledged as the original creators. Sharing people's work in other ways without getting permission or paying for it is illegal, so always use the proper sources.

Productivity and Organization

Like in the offline world, organization is crucial for working efficiently. Searching for an item in a messy room is challenging, and clutter can distract you from focusing. Similarly, your digital life becomes much more manageable when it's well-organized!

Using Cloud Storage

Over the past decade, cloud storage has become a standard way to store digital data. Files stored in the cloud can be accessed easily from any internet-connected computer, allowing instant sharing without requiring direct computer-to-computer connections.

Before cloud storage, data had to be stored locally — on individual computers — and shared by file transfer or email. Using the cloud makes it much easier and faster to collaborate on projects, and saves storage space for individuals. Many cloud storage services exist, like Google Drive, Dropbox, and Microsoft OneDrive. They all work in a similar way: You upload your files to the cloud, where they are stored securely, and then you can access them from anywhere with an internet connection.

One popular cloud storage example is Google Photos. If you sync it with your phone, any photo you take automatically uploads to Google Photos, where it's stored on Google's servers. You can access these photos anytime and from anywhere through your account.

ORGANIZING DIGITAL FILES

Managing digital files is an ongoing job, and organizing as you go is best. Once you get into the habit, it'll be with you for life. The following tips will help you get started.

How you create folders, use tags, and do other similar things will depend on your operating system (Windows, MacOS, Linux). Here are a few general pointers.

1. **Create folders:** Make folders to group related files together so you know where to look for them. You can even use different colors for different subjects or types of files.

2. **Use descriptive file and folder names:** Although you might think you'll remember what's in a particular file or folder, you will likely forget after a while. Use names that tell you what's inside — you'll thank yourself later.

3. **Sort and delete regularly:** Take some time now and then to review your files and remove old ones if you don't need them.

What Is the Cloud?

"The cloud" is a simple way of describing the huge network of computers that makes the Internet run. Although the term suggests that "the cloud" doesn't have much of a physical existence, in reality, all the information is held in huge server farms (a special type of computer). When many of these computers are linked together, they can do things that individual computers can't.

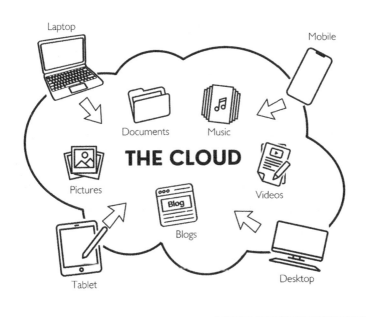

4. **Use tags and metadata:** File tags are information about a file that helps you categorize and organize it more easily.

5. **Organize your bookmarks:** Using folders and subfolders for your browser bookmarks makes it much easier to find them when you want to.

Backing Up

Have you ever spilled a drink on your computer — or seen someone else do it? If so, you probably heard, "I hope you've got a backup!" Having a backup means keeping extra copies of your important files. That way, if one set gets damaged — say, by a soda spill — you have another set safe and ready to go.

It's crucial to back up your files regularly. This involves copying them to a different type of storage, so you have at least two copies in separate locations. If one gets damaged, the other is still available. For example, you might keep your main files on your laptop, back them up to a cloud service like OneDrive, and use a USB stick for an additional layer of security. This protects your data if your laptop gets soaked in soda or eaten by a dog.

Downloading and Sharing Files

Files can hold nasty surprises, such as viruses, so it's crucial that you only download files from trusted online sources. It's a good idea to ask an adult before downloading anything so that they can check the source. If you're being offered something for free, be suspicious. "Free" often comes with a hidden cost!

It's also very important not to plug anything into your computer that you find or that was given to you by someone you don't know. Viruses can be passed from USB sticks and other devices. If someone needs to share a file with you, ask them to use the cloud. Likewise, if you need to share files with someone else, use cloud storage or email.

DIGITAL COMMERCE: HOW TO BE A SAVVY ONLINE SHOPPER

Online shopping makes it simple to get virtually any item you like from anywhere in the world. The Internet is not only the world's biggest library, but also the world's biggest department store! In one afternoon, you can choose a new outfit, purchase school supplies for the coming term, stock up on Japanese food ingredients, and more. It's like having every shop you could ever want to visit, all in one place.

Mastering the Art of Online Shopping

Of course, as with the rest of life online, digital commerce requires a bit of know-how to get the most out of it. In this chapter, you'll learn everything you need to know about digital commerce, online shopping, and making purchases online.

There is a dizzying variety of online shopping stores and platforms available. If you think about the many stores in the biggest shopping mall, that doesn't even come close.

WHERE TO SHOP ONLINE

Some shopping websites are online versions of bricks-and-mortar stores, such as Target, Best Buy, and The Home Depot. Others are huge online-only platforms where you can find pretty much anything. Some popular online shopping platforms to explore include:

Amazon
- **Good for:** Pretty much anything you can think of. Amazon carries a wide range of products, from electronics, clothing, and books to groceries and more.

- **Key features:** Huge selection of goods and sellers. Prime membership includes faster shipping and access to Prime Video. Robust customer review system. Use voice commands to shop with Amazon Echo.

eBay

- **Good for:** Many new and used items, including clothes, electronics, collectibles, and more, at price points to suit various budgets.

- **Key features:** Auctions and "Buy It Now" listings. Huge range of items from individual sellers and businesses. Rare finds and vintage items.

Etsy

- **Good for:** Handmade, vintage, unique jewelry, clothing, art, and crafts.

- **Key features:** Items from independent sellers and small businesses. There are lots of one-of-a-kind finds in this community-driven marketplace.

Depop

- **Good for:** Pre-loved fashion items, vintage clothing, accessories, and rare finds.

- **Key features:** Users sell and buy items directly to and from each other. Lots of rare and unique finds. Huge range of items and prices. Strong focus on community.

Steam

- **Good for:** Video games of all kinds, from AAA releases to small indie games.

- **Key features:** Huge variety of games. Lots of different price points. Easy for creators to sell their games. Works across different operating systems.

MARKETPLACES VS E-COMMERCE SITES

It's important to distinguish between online marketplaces and e-commerce sites when shopping online, as they offer different shopping experiences.

Online Marketplace	E-Commerce Sites
Lots of individual sellers or small businesses.	Usually owned and operated by one company selling directly to customers.
The marketplace deals with payments and sometimes handles delivery and customer service.	The company handles everything, from payments to customer service and delivery.
Sellers have little control over how their "storefront" looks. The marketplace controls everything.	The company has complete control over how its website looks.
Examples: Ebay, Amazon Marketplace, Etsy, Depop	Examples: Nike.com, Apple.com

Payment Methods

Once you've found what you're looking for, you have to pay for it.

There are many different ways to pay for online purchases, each with advantages and disadvantages. Here, you'll find a brief explanation of some of the most commonly used payment methods.

Credit Cards

Credit cards let you pay with money you borrow from the issuing bank. Rather than money coming from your account, the bank lends you the money for the purchase. Then, you pay it back over a specific period.

Pros:

- **Fraud protection:** Very strong protection in case of fraudulent payments. If you notice a charge you didn't authorize, or if the item you receive is faulty, the credit card company can help you recover your money.

- **Rewards and benefits**: Credit card companies provide cashback, discounts, travel miles, and other perks to encourage spending. These rewards can lead to savings, good deals, and occasional freebies.

- **Build up credit history:** A good credit history makes getting products like loans and mortgages easier when you're older. Using a credit card responsibly is a simple way to build your credit history.

- **No-interest period:** If you pay off your credit card debt within a specified time, you might not pay interest. This can be a useful way to purchase large-ticket items you can't afford outright, such as a new TV.

Cons:

- **Interest charges:** Credit cards charge interest on unpaid balances after the no-interest period ends. This means you'll pay more than the original purchase amount if you haven't paid it off in time.

- **Risk of overspending:** It can be tempting to spend more than you can afford with a credit card, as you don't see the money coming out of your bank account.

- **Fees:** Some credit cards have extra fees attached, making them very expensive.

- **Debt:** Credit cards are a form of debt. If you don't keep up with your payments, the interest rate can increase and spiral out of control. This can also affect your credit score, which means you may be unable to borrow money for things like a house or car when you're older.

What Is Interest?

When you borrow money from a bank, you must pay it back with a little extra. This extra is called interest, and is how the bank earns money from the loan. Interest rates are usually a percentage known as the annual percentage rate (APR), which indicates how much interest you'll pay over a year.

Debit Cards

Debit cards let you pay for things with money directly from your bank account. You must have money available in the account to use a debit card. If you don't have the money, your purchase will be declined.

Pros:

- **Debt-free:** The money comes straight from your bank account, so no debt or borrowing is involved.

- **No interest:** No debt means no interest!

- **Convenient:** Debit cards are accepted everywhere and are quick and easy to use.

Cons:

- **Weaker fraud protection:** It can be harder to reverse fraudulent payments than with a credit card.

- **Limited rewards:** Most debit cards don't come with rewards or cashback.

- **Overdraft fees:** If you spend more money than you have in your account, you'll likely be charged an overdraft fee.

Digital Wallets (PayPal, Apple Pay, Google Pay, etc.)

Digital wallets, like Apple Pay or PayPal, combine the convenience of debit cards with the security of credit cards. When you open a digital wallet account, you enter your payment card details. After that, you never have to enter those details again to make payments — you simply use your wallet.

Pros:

- **Security and privacy:** The digital wallet stores and protects your information. This means you don't have to enter and share your card details every time you make an online purchase. Digital wallets use the latest technology, making fraudulent charges much more unlikely.

- **Convenience:** Making payments is easy and smooth, no matter where you shop online. Add your items to the cart, choose your digital wallet at checkout, and the payment will be made using the card linked to your wallet. It works on many websites and apps, making shopping faster and more secure.

Cons:

- **Transaction fees:** You might be charged for particular types of transactions, like sending money abroad.

- **Technological dependence:** Digital wallets work with devices like smartphones and smartwatches. They cannot be used without those devices.

- **Ease of use:** Digital wallets make spending incredibly convenient, but sometimes they're almost too easy to use. It can be tempting to tap, pay, and not think about the money being spent, which might lead to overspending.

Buy Now Pay Later (BNPL) Services (Splitit, Klarna, Four, Flex etc.)

BNPL services allow you to purchase and receive items and pay for them later, often in installments (the cost is divided into several smaller parts).

For instance, imagine you find a jacket you love that costs $100, but you only have $20. Using BNPL, you don't have to pay the whole amount up front. Instead, you can divide the payment into smaller parts (often interest-free) over a certain period. So, if you get $20 every month, you could choose to spread the cost over five months.

Pros:

- **Pay in installments:** BNPL makes purchases more affordable in the short term by splitting payments into smaller parts.

- **Interest-free period:** These services often charge no interest on payments for a fixed period.

- **Convenient:** It's usually quick and easy to get approved for BNPL services.

Cons:

- **BNPL is debt:** Remember, using BNPL means taking on a short-term loan. Essentially, you are borrowing money to make your purchase.

- **Fees and penalties:** Missing payments or defaulting (stopping paying altogether) will lead to extra costs, which can spiral out of control.

- **High interest rates:** Many BNPL services charge very high interest rates outside the interest-free period. If you miss payments, the purchase cost can significantly increase, sometimes making you pay much more than the item's original price.

- **Risk of overspending:** BNPL makes it tempting to buy more than you can afford, since you don't have to pay the full amount immediately.

- **Promotes unnecessary spending:** BNPL services are often linked to fast fashion and other impulse-buy sites, encouraging spending on things you might not need.

👍 PROS	👎 CONS
Credit Cards • Fraud protection • Rewards and benefits • Build up credit history	• High potential interest charges • Risk of overspending • Fees • Debt
Debit Cards • Debt-free • No interest • Convenient	• Weaker fraud protection • Limited rewards • Overdraft fee
E-wallets • Security & privacy • Convenient	• Transaction fees • Technological dependence • May be too easy to use & spend
Buy Now Pay Later • Pay in installments • Interest-free period • Convenient	• BNPL is debt • Fees & penalties • High interest rates • Risk of overspending • Promotes unnecessary spending

UNDERSTANDING DIFFERENT PAYMENT TYPES

There are several different ways to make payments online. The simplest is a single payment for a one-off purchase, while more complex types include subscriptions and recurring fees. Understanding what kind of payment you're signing up for before purchasing online is essential.

Single Purchases

Single purchases are a one-off transaction where you pay for a product or service when you purchase it. Once you've paid and the transaction is complete, you have a legal right to the product or service. You'll either receive it straight away (in the case of a digital purchase) or your item will be shipped to you. For example, when you buy a game through Steam, you choose the game, enter your details, click "Pay," and the game is yours to download.

In-App Purchases and Virtual Currencies

In-app purchases are purchases you make in a particular app or platform for use within that environment. Platforms often use their own "virtual currency," which you have to buy with real currency or earn in the app. For instance, in Fortnite, you use real money to buy the virtual currency "V-bucks," which you can use to purchase in-game items.

It's vital to think carefully before making in-app purchases. These systems are designed to encourage users to spend more, and it's easy to run up a huge bill. Always check with a trusted adult before making any in-app purchases, pay attention to what you are clicking on, and avoid linking payment accounts to apps, if possible.

Subscriptions and Recurring Payments

Recurring payments and subscriptions are purchases that happen automatically at a specific time, usually once per week, month, or year. They are used for ongoing access to products or services, such as streaming services or subscription boxes, and continue until the user cancels the subscription. These types of payments are increasingly used for software such as Microsoft Office and Adobe Photoshop.

"Buy now pay later" services also use recurring payments, but the payments end when the total owed is paid off.

Subscriptions are a simple way to make recurring payments for products and services you want to use regularly. However, it's easy to end up with many subscriptions you don't need or want, or find yourself paying out more than you can afford.

To avoid oversubscription issues, regularly review your subscriptions and cancel any that no longer work for you. Use phone alerts to remind you what payments are scheduled and when, and check bank statements regularly for any subscriptions you've forgotten about.

Understanding Digital Currencies

Digital currencies, often known as cryptocurrencies (or "crypto" for short), are modern money that only exists in digital form. They are different from regular (or "fiat") money in that they are not controlled by any centralized authority, but instead are "decentralized" and secured by blockchain technology.

Decentralization

While the Federal Reserve controls the US dollar, the most famous digital currency, Bitcoin, is not controlled by any one organization — it's decentralized. Every transaction with Bitcoin is recorded on the blockchain (basically an enormous list) for everyone to see. The idea is that this keeps the system transparent and secure.

Using Cryptocurrency

People use cryptocurrencies like Bitcoin to send money online and occasionally to pay for goods and services offline. Many view them as alternative investments, similar to commodities like gold or silver, rather than as traditional financial currencies for everyday purchases.

What Are the Risks?

Using or investing in digital currencies is very risky due to their extreme volatility. The value of these currencies can fluctuate dramatically — a single cryptocurrency "coin" might be worth $50 one day and just $1 the next, meaning if you bought it at $50 and sold it at $1, you would lose $49.

Digital currency regulation is still in its early stages globally, and it's unclear how the laws and rules around them will develop. In some regions, these currencies are even banned, raising doubts about the practicality of using digital currency for most people at this time.

SECURING YOUR TRANSACTIONS AND RECOGNIZING SCAMS

It's crucial to ensure your transactions are secure when shopping online. This means keeping your payment information hidden to prevent it from being stolen during the transaction, protecting you from potential fraud. Unsafe transactions can allow thieves to use your information for their purchases or sell it to others.

Shopping websites use various methods to protect their customers. The most important step is to stay alert and ensure the website uses the best security technology. Once you know what you're looking for, it's easy to check. If a site doesn't appear secure, stay away. No item is worth the risk of a scam or theft!

When making purchases online, here are key practices to keep you safe:

1. **Shop at reputable sites:** Stick to well-known retailers and research unfamiliar websites before purchasing. If in doubt, don't use them.

2. **Check for the "S" in URLs:** Shop only on sites that show "https://" in the URL and a padlock symbol in the address bar, indicating a secure TLS certificate.

3. **Use secure payment methods:** Credit cards and reputable third-party payment services like PayPal offer strong protection against fraud.

4. **Enable two-factor authentication (2FA):** This adds an extra layer of security by requiring a special one-time code each time a payment is made.

What Is a TLS Certificate?

Without getting too deep into technical talk, TLS certificates (often known as SSL certificates) show that a site is safe to visit. With a TLS certificate, you can be sure that any data sent through the website is encrypted (scrambled into a tough-to-crack code) and hidden from anyone who might want to steal it.

Your browser automatically checks for a TLS certificate when you visit a website, so you don't need to do anything. Look for the "S" and the padlock in the address bar. If you get a warning saying the certificate is out of date or not valid, stay away from the site.

Unfortunately, the online world is also full of scammers looking to make an easy dollar at your expense, so being vigilant is key.

1. **Check for authenticity:** Legitimate businesses pay attention to their online presence. Spelling mistakes and poor-quality images are big warning signs.

2. **Do your research:** Investigate sellers thoroughly, check customer support details and read customer reviews,

especially negative ones. Also, look for additional ratings on review sites like Trustpilot.

3. **Protect your personal information:** Never give out sensitive information like passwords, banking details, or Social Security Numbers.

4. **If it seems too good to be true...:** It probably is. Be skeptical of offers that are too good to be true. They are usually scams in disguise.

5. **Stay vigilant:** Treat being online like walking on the street — stay alert and cautious. Report anything suspicious to the authorities and stay up-to-date on scams and best security practices.

Making Informed Decisions

Successful online shopping requires understanding product descriptions, reviews, and terms and conditions. Without this basic knowledge, making informed decisions can be challenging. As with many topics in this book, these skills are applicable in various situations, both online and offline. It's well worth paying them some attention!

Finding the Best Deals

With so many choices available online, finding the best deal can feel overwhelming. However, there are effective strategies to streamline your search. Use these tips to find great deals, every time. Always exercise caution and stay alert. While there are genuine bargains out there, remember: if it seems too good to be true, it probably is!

1. **Use price comparison sites:** These websites, such as Shopzilla, Google Shopping, and PriceGrabber, simplify comparing prices across different platforms. They allow you to use filters to refine your search and provide real-time information to ensure you see the most up-to-date prices.

2. **Learn to search effectively:** Sharpen your search skills to pinpoint the best deals. Be specific with your search terms, include words like "discount" or "sale," and use special search operators like quotation marks to search like a pro.

Top Tip

For big-ticket items, search using the manufacturer's serial number instead of the product name. This can help you compare prices more accurately across different sellers.

3. **Time it right:** Shop during sales seasons, such as Black Friday, Cyber Monday, and end-of-season sales, to take advantage

of the best deals, especially on electronics and clothing. Also, buying off-season, like purchasing summer clothes in winter, will often save you money.

4. **Use vouchers and discounts:** Sites like RetailMeNot, Coupons.com, and Honey offer discount codes for a wide range of products. Check the voucher details, apply it at checkout, and save.

5. **Take advantage of loyalty programs and cashback offers:** Many sites and platforms have loyalty programs that offer savings or rewards on regular purchases. Signing up for email alerts can also provide exclusive discounts. Cashback sites like TopCashback can also help you get money back on your purchases.

COMPARING PRODUCTS

When deciding whether to make a purchase, it's crucial to consider various aspects and compare multiple options. Here's what to keep in mind:

Features and Specifications

Ensure the product meets your specific needs. For instance, if you need a table for a certain corner, confirm the dimensions to fit that space.

Focus on essential features. For instance, if you're buying a smartphone, these might include a foldable design and an AI-assisted camera.

These are the product's features. Specifications include details like the size, weight, and color. These will help you understand the product better and determine whether it matches your requirements.

Value for Money

The cheapest item isn't always the best choice. While everyone loves a good deal, it's essential to consider the overall value an item offers. Ask yourself: How long will it last? Is it reliable? Can it be repaired?

Very cheap items, especially electronics, may have a short lifespan and often cannot be repaired. Although the initial cost is lower, you may end up replacing them sooner, which can be more expensive over time. These items are also terrible for the environment. They are hard to recycle, so they often end up in landfills once they break.

When shopping for clothing, consider the "cost per wear" value. For example, a jacket that costs twice as much might be better value if it lasts three times longer. Always consider the durability and longevity of the item.

Customer Reviews

Always read reviews of an item before making a purchase. Look for both positive and negative points, and pay special attention to reviews from customers who used the product in ways similar to how you plan to use it. Keep in mind that not all reviews or reviewers are trustworthy. Despite this, reviews can still provide a useful general sense of a product's quality.

Expert Opinions

There are lots of websites and videos where experts test and review products. If you're considering a technical or high-value item, it's a good idea to explore these resources to get expert insights. However, be cautious — some review sites earn money from the companies whose products they review, so it's important to check the credibility of the reviewers before fully trusting their opinions.

Return Policies and Warranties

Always check the return policy and warranty terms before buying a product. These are crucial for knowing what to do if the item fails to meet your expectations. Beware of cheap items from faraway places; it can be expensive and complicated to return an item, and there may be no warranty.

Deciphering Reviews

Customer reviews are invaluable when deciding whether to buy a product. But not all reviews are equal. When evaluating an item, consider both the positive and negative feedback. It's tempting to overlook negative reviews if you're attracted to a product, but that's not usually a good idea.

Spotting Fake Reviews

Some sellers and businesses pay people to write fake reviews of their products, or negative reviews about competitors' products. It's challenging to spot fake reviews, but here are some things to look out for:

- **Repetitive patterns:** If reviews share the same pattern, details, or similar overly positive or negative comments, they might be fake.

- **Single review accounts:** Reviewers who have posted only one review or multiple reviews for the same company are suspicious.

- **Excessively positive or negative:** Generic reviews that are excessively positive or negative without clear details about the product could also be fake.

These signs suggest that the reviews may not be genuine.

Verified Purchase Reviews

To combat fake reviews, many sites mark reviews as "Verified Purchase" to confirm the reviewer actually bought the item. While these reviews are generally more trustworthy, be aware that some companies pay individuals to purchase and review products, so they are not foolproof.

CALCULATING THE TOTAL COST OF A PURCHASE

Before making a purchase, it's crucial to understand its total cost. While most websites display this information clearly, it's wise to calculate it independently as well, just to be certain.

1. **Check the item price:** The base price of the item is typically prominently displayed.

2. **Include shipping costs:** While shipping may sometimes be free, often it must be added to the item's cost. Shipping fees are usually found on a dedicated page of the site or in the terms and conditions.

3. **Account for taxes:** Additional taxes might apply to your purchase. Check this information and add the appropriate amount to your total.

4. **Apply any discounts:** If you have a discount voucher or code, deduct the amount or percentage from the total.

5. **Calculate the total:** Combine the item's price, shipping costs, and taxes, then subtract any applicable discounts. The final number is the total cost of your purchase.

So, **Total Cost = Price of Item + Shipping Costs + Taxes–Discounts**

Always double-check everything before you make your purchase!

After Purchase — Support and Problem Solving

Shopping online is often a smooth and trouble-free experience. But sometimes, things go wrong. Because there's no physical store to return an item to or visible staff to talk to, it can be hard to know what to do. Remember that reputable shopping sites should deal with you fairly and honestly.

YOUR CONSUMER RIGHTS

When shopping from a trustworthy online retailer, you generally have similar legal protections as when buying from a physical store. These protections include your right to return faulty items, cancel certain types of orders within a specific timeframe, dispute incorrect or unauthorized charges, and expect fair treatment and privacy protection from businesses.

The specific rules and regulations depend on your location and the site from which you've made your purchase. Understanding these rights is crucial for making informed purchasing decisions.

USING SELF-HELP RESOURCES

If you need help with a product, start by exploring the self-help resources available. Most online retailers provide FAQs and tutorials on their websites — these can be great for resolving common problems.

User forums can also be handy. The communities around certain products or companies often know more and offer better solutions than official customer support. Before posting a new question in a forum, make sure to check if it has already been addressed; chances are, someone else has faced the same issue!

REACHING OUT FOR HELP

If you can't resolve an issue using the self-help resources, your next step is to contact customer support. You can find contact information on the business's website.

If the business offers live chat, it's a quick way to get help. Emailing customer support is a good option if you're not in a hurry. For direct interaction, consider using phone support if available.

When contacting support, be prepared with all the details about your issue. This includes your order number, product name or number, any error messages, and a detailed description of the problem. Providing complete information helps the support team resolve your issue more efficiently.

Managing Money and Online Banking

Online banking allows you to access and manage your money electronically. It makes sending money, paying for items, and moving money between your accounts quick and easy. You can access your online banking accounts 24 hours a day, seven days a week — as long as there's an Internet connection — making it incredibly convenient. Additionally, modern banking platforms use the most up-to-date encryption methods, ensuring your transactions are safe and secure.

HOW TO SET UP AN ONLINE BANK ACCOUNT

Setting up an online bank account is straightforward but usually requires the help of an adult.

1. **Choose a reputable bank:** Start by researching banks and financial service providers in your area. Consider their security measures, customer reviews, and the services they offer. Check whether the bank operates solely online or also has physical branches, which can be useful for face-to-face interactions.

2. **Sign up for online banking:** Visit the bank's website and follow the instructions to sign up. You'll need an adult to assist you, along with personal details like your name, address, and Social Security Number. Depending on the bank, you may

need to open a bank account first, or you might be able to sign up for an account and online banking simultaneously.

3. **Create a strong password:** It's crucial to use a strong password for all your accounts, especially for banking. Use a mix of upper and lowercase letters, numbers, and special characters. Refer to the password creation guide in Chapter 1.

4. **Download the app:** For mobile access, download your bank's app and log in with your details. Do this over a secure Wi-Fi connection, not in a public place. Once set up, your online bank account is ready to use.

FINDING BALANCE: HOW TO MANAGE SCREEN TIME AND WELL-BEING

The Internet has become such an important part of everyday life that it often seems more appealing than the offline world. It's easy to get swept up in the digital world and overlook the incredible experiences the offline world has to offer! In reality, many of life's most important moments take place away from the screen with friends and family, outdoors, and in nature.

The Quest for Digital Equilibrium

You've probably heard the sayings "too much of a good thing" and "moderation in all things." These expressions emphasize the importance of balance. Having a good thing all the time — even when it is brilliant, like ice cream or the Internet — can lose its appeal and make for an unbalanced life.

Having a mixture of interests and activities is essential to prevent this imbalance. Just as a varied diet is crucial for physical health, engaging in a range of activities is beneficial for overall well-being. While the idea of having ice cream for every meal might seem tempting, it wouldn't be healthy, and it might also — believe it or not — get boring pretty quickly. The same applies to all aspects of life, including spending time online. It's healthy and useful in the right dose, but too much is just that — too much.

THE BENEFITS OF BALANCE

Maintaining a healthy balance between online and offline time is crucial for every part of your life, from mental health to personal relationships. Finding the right balance can significantly improve your quality of life.

Spending too much time online has been linked to poorer mental and physical health in young people. By balancing this with offline experiences, you can enjoy "real-world" pleasures and get the best of both worlds.

Managing Your Screen Time

You've probably heard a lot of talk about "screen time," especially concerning the amount young people spend on screens and whether it's too much. However, it's important to recognize that not all screen time is created equal, and whether it's "good" or "bad" is not a simple issue.

> ### What Is Screen Time?
>
> Screen time is the time people spend looking at electronic devices with screens. This includes smartphones, games consoles, TVs, tablets, cinema screens, and anything else with a screen.

There are three basic types of screen time:

- **Educational:** Screen time spent on activities where you're learning something. This includes schoolwork, language apps like Duolingo, or doing research.

- **Recreational:** Time spent on entertainment. Watching TV, playing video games, and scrolling through social media without interacting much are all examples of recreational screen time.

- **Social:** Time spent communicating directly with other people. Things like video calls, messaging through apps, and interacting with people through social media are social screen time.

THE IMPACT OF TOO MUCH SCREEN TIME

There's nothing intrinsically wrong with screen time. As part of a balanced lifestyle, it can play an important role in learning, socializing, and communicating. However, excessive screen use can have negative consequences, mainly because other aspects of life get ignored or forgotten.

Negative effects of screen time include:

- **Poor sleep:** Using screens before bed can disrupt sleep, making it difficult to fall asleep and stay asleep. Lack of quality sleep can negatively affect mental and physical health.

- **Physical health problems:** Sitting for long periods can harm your bones and muscles and increase the risk of obesity. Staring at screens for too long can also strain your eyes.

- **Mental health problems:** Rates of depression, anxiety, and stress are on the rise among young people. Although they are not solely caused by screen time, spending too much time on screens, especially on social media, can lead to less interaction with others, heightening feelings of loneliness and worsening mental health concerns.

- **Weak social skills:** Not engaging in enough face-to-face conversations can weaken your ability to communicate and collaborate with others, impacting your social skills. Social skills are like muscles — they need exercise to stay strong!

SETTING HEALTHY LIMITS

There's no need to panic about screen time, but setting limits and boundaries for yourself and encouraging your friends and family to do the same is a good idea. Use these tips to help you create a healthy balance between online and offline time.

1. **Create a weekly screen schedule:** A schedule can help you manage your screen time and maintain a healthy balance. Decide on a schedule that suits you, with specific time slots for different screen time activities. For example, consider limiting evening screen time to one hour before dinner.

2. **Use screen time monitoring apps:** There are many apps available that can tell you how long you spend on your devices and how you spend that time. Many digital devices have these features built-in — check the settings for "Digital Wellbeing Controls" or similar. These apps and features can help you understand your screen time and stay accountable.

3. **Establish screen-free zones:** Work with your family to choose specific parts of your home as screen-free zones to encourage more face-to-face interaction. Bedrooms and dining rooms are a good choice.

4. **Lead by example:** Modeling healthy screen time behavior will help others do it, too. Encourage your friends and family to find a healthy balance and suggest activities you can do together that don't involve screens.

How to Create a Personal Screen Time Plan

Making a plan is a great way to create a healthy balance between screen time and screen-free time. It will help you understand what you want from your screen time and what you'd like to focus more on off-screen.

Ask yourself these questions to help you build a plan tailored to your life.

- **How much screen time do I get currently?** Use monitoring apps or features to track your screen time. If you can't use an app, use a timer and a notebook. Be honest with yourself and record it all.

- **What do I do with my screen time?** Use those apps to understand precisely how you spend your time online. Again, be honest with yourself. You might be surprised how long you scroll through Instagram or other social media feeds!

- **What do I want to do with my screen time?** Work out your priorities for screen time. You probably have schoolwork, friends you want to speak with, or other things you want to do online. Make those the things you use most of your screen time for.

- **What's my schedule?** Based on your answers to the previous questions, establish a schedule that includes limits for each type of screen activity. Even a flexible schedule should have clear boundaries to help manage your screen time effectively.

- **What would I like to do more of?** Consider activities you enjoy that don't involve screens, such as spending time with friends, playing sports, or reading. Plan to use the time you save from reduced screen use for these interests.

MANAGING NOTIFICATIONS AND DISTRACTIONS

App notifications can be useful, but too many can become overwhelming and distract you from important tasks or conversations. Here are some tips to help manage them.

1. **Switch them off:** Most apps allow you to turn off or limit their notifications. Dive into your app settings and turn off notifications for apps you don't need constant updates

from. Just remember to leave important ones, like banking apps, active.

2. **Use "do not disturb"**: Mealtimes, bedtime, and deep conversations with friends are ideal times to use your device's "do not disturb" function, which silences all but the most urgent notifications. Your device will continue to function normally — it just won't interrupt you.

3. **Try "focus mode."** Similar to "do not disturb," "focus mode" quietens your device so that you can concentrate on other things. Depending on the situation, you can customize it to allow notifications from certain apps or contacts.

4. **Out of sight, out of mind**: When you're not using your phone or tablet, place it somewhere out of sight. This reduces distractions, and the temptation to check it frequently diminishes when it's not within easy reach.

Time for a Digital Detox?

Spending too much time online or glued to screens can lead to some serious downsides. It's vital to monitor its impact on you and consider taking a break if digital life becomes overwhelming.

RECOGNIZING WHEN SCREEN TIME IS BECOMING A PROBLEM

Sometimes, you might feel the effects of too much screen time, but other times, the signs are less noticeable. Knowing the symptoms of addiction and digital burnout is crucial. Here are some red flags to watch for:

- **Preoccupation with screens**: Constantly thinking about screen time and struggling to focus on anything else.

- **Neglecting responsibilities**: Putting off essential things to spend more time on your devices/gaming/watching TV.

- **Losing control**: Feeling like you can't stop checking or using your devices, even if you want to or have tried to.

- **Using for longer than intended**: Losing time and neglecting other parts of life by spending more time on your devices than you mean to.

- **Feeling bad, mentally or physically**: If you notice any decline in how you feel mentally or physically, it could be a sign that you're spending too much time on your devices.

SIGNS OF DIGITAL BURNOUT

Ignoring signs that digital use and screen time are causing problems can lead to digital burnout. Burnout is a serious health condition in which the body and mind go into a kind of exhausted shock after being exposed to stress for a long time. Don't ignore these symptoms if you notice them in yourself or if others notice them in you.

Speak to a healthcare professional, or, if that isn't an option, to a trusted adult, then take steps to reduce your screen time. Use the strategies in this chapter to help manage your digital exposure.

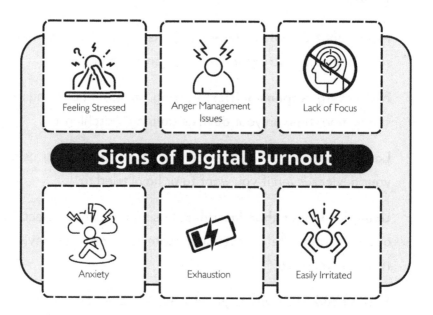

Symptoms of burnout include.

- **Feeling exhausted:** Feeling very tired, even after getting enough sleep, with little or no energy for basic activities.

- **Lack of motivation:** Losing interest in things you once enjoyed and feeling indifferent about many aspects of life.

- **Struggles concentrating:** Difficulty focusing on routine tasks and everyday conversations.

- **Mood swings:** Sudden mood swings for no apparent reason, or frequently feeling cross, angry, or irritable.

- **Physical symptoms:** Headaches, eye strain, sore muscles, digestive issues, and other physical symptoms without an obvious cause.

- **Avoiding people:** Not wanting to be around others and avoiding social situations.

- **Problems sleeping:** Difficulty falling asleep or staying asleep, frequent waking during the night, bad dreams, and feeling tired even after sleeping.

DIGITAL DETOX STRATEGIES

A "digital detox" is a great way to take action when you notice you're spending too much time with devices and screens. When trying digital detox strategies, it's a good idea to tell other people you trust so they can help you and offer support. They might even join you!

Here are some simple ideas to try with your digital detox.

Try Screen-Free Zones

Designate areas like bedrooms, dining rooms, and family rooms as screen-free zones. Eliminating devices from the bedroom will improve your sleep. Additionally, you might find that conversations and activities in these screen-free areas are more enjoyable and engaging when people aren't glued to their phones.

Use Your Screen Schedule

You might not want to (or be able to) stop using devices completely, instead, consider establishing a structured screen schedule to help regulate your screen time. You'll need self-control here, but remember, it's for your own good!

Create Tech-Free Habits

Introduce small, enjoyable habits that don't involve using screens into your day. Whether having breakfast without your phone, writing in a notebook on the way to school, or stepping outside into nature, these activities contribute to a more fulfilling real-world experience.

Get Outside

Green spaces, fresh air, and sunlight are all proven mood boosters. Spending time outdoors is the perfect way to get offline. Hiking, biking, playing sports, or simply walking around are all great ways to improve your mood and reduce stress. You don't have to be out in the countryside (although it's great if you can be) — even a walk around the block will positively affect your body and mind.

Embrace Analog Activities

Explore the endless array of enjoyable and engaging activities that don't rely on devices or screens. From crafting and learning a musical instrument to journaling and photography. Not only is it fun to try new things and work on skills, but you'll also often have something to show for it!

Prioritize the People in the Room

Have you ever been talking with someone, and they suddenly get a notification on their phone and immediately break off the conversation to check it? It's annoying, right? Phones and notifications are designed to attract attention — and they do. But ignoring real people in favor of our devices can be annoying and hurtful. Over time, it can lead to weaker, less fulfilling relationships.

Pay attention to the people in the room. Listen to them when they speak, and concentrate on giving thoughtful replies. Keep your phone out of the conversation, and don't shy away from interacting because it's easier to look at a screen — social skills take practice, and if you don't use them, you'll lose them!

Healthy Habits Beyond the Screen

A healthy, balanced lifestyle isn't just about controlling your screen time. It's essential to consider other aspects of well-being as well! Building healthy habits from a young age is a wonderful way to increase your chances of enjoying a long, happy, healthy life — and who doesn't want that?

PHYSICAL ACTIVITY

Humans are designed to move. Staying active keeps bodies and minds strong and healthy, so getting as much physical activity as possible is important. Try these tips to help you increase your daily movement:

1. **Move often:** Whatever you're doing in your day, try to find ways to incorporate some movement. If you've been sitting for a while, walk around for a minute. Do some stretches while watching TV or working at your computer. Walk up the stairs instead of using the elevator. Look out for ways to move more in daily life.

2. **Do things you enjoy:** Walking, swimming, soccer, flying a kite — it doesn't matter what you do; what matters is that you enjoy it. Try out different activities until you find something you love. It doesn't have to be a sport. All kinds of movement count — even dancing around your bedroom!

3. **Set goals:** Goals make it easier to cultivate good habits. Try setting a goal like 30 minutes per day of continuous movement and see where it takes you. Update your goals when needed, and keep them realistic so you don't set yourself up for disappointment.

4. **Make a schedule:** Schedules help you achieve your goals and do more with your time. Try scheduling a daily movement session at a sensible time and sticking to it.

5. **Get other people involved:** Exercising with others can be more fun than going it alone, so round up some friends and get moving!

NUTRITION AND SLEEP

Food and sleep have a massive influence on overall health. Prioritizing healthy eating and sleeping will help you develop good habits and set you up for success, so follow these tips.

1. **Eat a balanced diet:** The more variety in your diet, the better. Eating many different foods, with a focus on vegetables, whole grains, and healthy fats, will give you all the nutrients you need.

2. **Eat mindfully:** Listen to your body — eat when you're hungry and stop when you've had enough. Pay attention to what you're eating and avoid doing other things at the same time, like watching TV or talking on the phone.

3. **Prioritize sleep:** Aim to get seven to nine hours of sleep per night. Sleeping is one of the body's essential processes, so don't put it off to do something else!

4. **Create a bedtime routine:** It can be easier to fall asleep when you have a routine that lets your body know it's bedtime. Taking a warm bath, getting into your pajamas, and reading a book for 15 minutes are all good ways to wind down.

5. **Avoid screen time before bed:** Using devices and watching TV can make the brain too alert to fall asleep. Try to avoid screens for at least an hour before bed.

MENTAL WELLNESS

Looking after your mind is just as important as looking after your body. The two are strongly connected, and you might find your mood improves when you look after your body. But there are also a few things we can do to nurture our minds.

1. **Avoid digital overload:** Use the tips and strategies in this chapter to help you manage your digital life.

2. **Practice your hobbies:** Doing things you enjoy is a great way to relax and unwind. Experiment with a mix of activities, and make sure some are offline.

3. **Connect with others:** Make time for the people in your life, even if you find social situations difficult. Connecting with others is one of the best ways to look after your mental health.

4. **Practice mindfulness:** Pay attention to the present moment and what you are doing. Notice the sensations and feelings. For instance, if you are drawing, concentrate on the pencil in your hand and the feeling as it touches the paper. Try not to obsess over the future or worry about the past. Instead, appreciate each moment as it comes.

5. **Get help if needed:** If you feel like you're struggling with your mental or physical health, tell a trusted adult. Don't keep it to yourself — people are ready and willing to help.

Embracing the Offline World

Now that you know how to strike a healthy digital balance, it's time to get out there and explore the offline world. There's so much to do and see! Sometimes, offline activities seem more difficult to get into than online ones. That's all the more reason to do them — when things are a challenge, that's when we learn and grow.

FINDING JOY OFF-SCREEN

Offline activities might not provide the immediate feel-good hit that online activities can. Still, over time, you'll likely find that they give you more fulfillment, enjoyment, and long-lasting pleasure. Here are a few ideas to get you started.

1. **Take your hobbies further**: Find ways to get deeper into whatever interests you. That could mean attending conventions, reading books, visiting museums, or talking with others who share your interests.

2. **Discover new interests**: Try new activities, even if you're not sure you'll like them. Sometimes, you'll be surprised! And you'll learn a lot about yourself with each new activity you try.

3. **Embrace uncertainty:** Embrace the unknown. For example, avoid looking at the menu online before you visit a new restaurant. When you go on a trip, walk around without using Google Maps. Try not to worry about not having everything planned out.

4. **Try volunteering:** Helping in the community is a great way to connect with others and feel more involved with your local area. Look for open days or welcome sessions with local groups that interest you.

SCREEN-FREE SOCIALIZING

Humans are social animals, and we thrive in the company of other people. But offline socializing can be nerve-racking when you're not used to it. The good news is that it gets easier with practice. If you're looking for ideas on how to up your offline socializing game, try these tips.

1. **Plan outdoor adventures:** Socializing is easier when there's a focus, so organize group trips into the great outdoors. You don't have to go far — the local park is fine. Just take some friends along!

2. **Attend local events:** Once you start looking, you'll find that most places have a lot going on. Local festivals, markets, music, and art events are perfect for exploring with friends and family and meeting new people.

3. **Host a game night:** Get your friends and family involved in a group game night. You could play board games, card games, physical games like charades, or a mixture of game types.

4. **Join clubs or groups:** Themed groups are an easy way to meet people who are interested in similar things. There are groups for everything you can imagine, from crochet to camping, so check out your local options.

Take Time in Nature

The sights, sounds, and smells of the outdoors affect the human body in ways scientists are only just beginning to understand. What we do know is that spending time in nature has many benefits, including improved mood, reduced stress and anxiety, and better quality sleep. Try these ideas to immerse yourself in nature.

1. **Take a nature walk:** Simply walking through a natural environment benefits the body. Watching the birds, counting the different kinds of plants and bugs, or just enjoying the feeling of the air on your skin — it's all good!

2. **Go camping or stargazing:** A starry night sky is a wonder everyone should see as often as possible. In towns and cities, a few stars might be visible, but the night sky is spectacular out in the wilderness. Camp in areas with as few buildings as possible. There are even "dark sky" reserves where you're guaranteed a fantastic view of the night sky.

3. **Get near the water:** Swimming, kayaking, or sunbathing on the shore (don't forget your sunscreen!) are all wonderful ways to enjoy nature. Explore your local seashore, lake, or pond; just check for safety information and take friends along with you!

4. **Tend your garden:** Growing and looking after plants is a rewarding way to spend time outdoors. If you have a garden at your house, ask if you can take ownership of a patch. Growing plants in pots on a balcony or indoors is just as much fun if you don't have a garden.

CONCLUSION

We've reached the end of this voyage of digital discovery. Take a moment to pat yourself on the back! If you don't remember everything you read, don't worry — you can dip into this book whenever you need to for a quick refresher.

Throughout this book, you've learned all about:

- The history of digital communication, how it came about, and why it matters.

- How to stay safe online, including how to spot scams and keep your bank account safe and secure.

- Netiquette, how to conduct yourself online, and look out for others.

- How to communicate effectively in different digital situations, from video calls to group chats.

- How to search, shop, and spot fake news successfully.

- How to stay healthy mentally and physically and find the right balance between online and offline.

To break it down, you might say that the three main takeaways of this book are:

- Respect yourself and other people online (and offline!).

- Keep your wits about you online (and offline!).

- Stay curious and keep learning.

WHAT'S NEXT?

Developing strong digital skills is one of the best gifts you can give yourself, and it's never too late or too early to start. These skills will stay with you for life, but it's important to practice to keep them sharp. Think of this book as the first step in a lifelong journey of digital understanding, and use it to build from as you grow.

To keep your digital skills in top shape, the best thing you can do is to keep working on them. Because the digital world moves on so quickly, it's pretty common to be up-to-date and on top of everything one minute and then feel lost and left behind the next.

To prevent this, follow tech trends and develop your skills wherever and whenever you can. Podcasts, newsletters, and forums are all great ways to stay up-to-date with what's going on. By incorporating your digital skills into your daily life responsibly and healthily, you'll set yourself up for success.

The End...and the Beginning

Now that you've got this incredible digital skills toolkit, it's time to use it! The next time you do anything online, think about how to use what you've learned to make your experience safer, more fun, and more valuable.

Why not share what you've learned with your friends and family? You might be surprised at how many people you can help with their digital skills. Remember that it is down to all of us to make the digital world a better place for everyone.

Good luck on your digital journey. May it be a long and fruitful one!

Your friend,
Ferne Bowe

BEMBERTON
BOOKS

THANKS
FOR READING MY
BOOK!

I truly hope you enjoyed the book and that the content is valuable now and in the future.

I would be grateful if you could leave an honest review or a star rating on Amazon.
(A star rating is just a couple of clicks away.)

By leaving a review, you'll help other parents discover this valuable resource for their children. Thank you!

To leave a review & help spread the word

SCAN
HERE

Made in United States
North Haven, CT
14 December 2024

62355145R00098